JESUS IS THE STAIRCASE

THE ONLY WAY TO HEAVEN

MATT RANKIN

Publish Authority

Jesus is the Staircase

ISBN 978-1-954000-61-2 (Paperback)
ISBN 978-1-954000-62-9 (eBook)
ISBN 978-1-954000-63-6 (Hardback)

Editor: Bob Laning
Cover design lead: Raeghan Rebstock
Interior design: Teresa Evans

Published 2024, by Publish Authority
300 Colonial Center Parkway, Suite 100
Roswell, GA 30076-4892 USA
PublishAuthority.com

Printed in the United States of America

CONTENTS

This book is dedicated to my darling wife, Nichole, and my magnificent son, David. Your amazing love and encouragement has blessed my life beyond words.
I love you both so much!

"Most assuredly, I say to you, hereafter you shall see heaven open, and the angels of God ascending and descending upon the Son of Man."

— JESUS CHRIST (JOHN 1:51 NKJV)

INTRODUCTION

Every person has two major problems, one is sin, and the other is death. There is only one person that could handle those two problems for us, and it is the one whom God sent. Jesus overcame sin at the cross, and He overcame death when He rose from the grave. Jesus is the only answer.

However, God did not send Jesus without first giving us the sure foundation of the prophecies and types and shadows of the Old Testament that would clearly and unmistakably identify Him as the Messiah and Savior whom the Father sent.

In Isaiah 46:9-10, the Bible tells us that God is the only one who can tell the end from the beginning. So, that is the way He chose to identify His Son to us, by telling the end from the beginning. Throughout the Old Testament, and ever since the world was created, God foretold of His Son through prophecies, types and shadows, numbers, patterns, and symbols that were given to His chosen people Israel, so that when Jesus came to this earth in the flesh, we would know that He is the Son of God.

Throughout the ages, step by step, here a little and there a little, God was unfolding His mighty plan of salvation, which was described in the Old Testament as a Staircase that reaches heaven. Through the Old Testament, God was showing us what Jesus would look like before He came so that when He came in the flesh, we would know He is the Staircase.

My hope as you read this book is that you will see how God was speaking of Jesus from the beginning. As you walk up the steps of the Staircase, my prayer is that you will know the heart of the Father and hear His voice calling you to choose Jesus, the only path to heaven.

Jesus said, "I Am the way, the truth, and the life. No one comes to the Father except through Me" (John 14:6 NKJV).

CHAPTER 1

PATHWAY OF DELIVERANCE

"Oh God, you are my God; early will I seek you;
my soul thirsts for you; my flesh longs for you
in a dry and thirsty land where there is no
water." (Psalm 63:1 NKJV)

PICTURE YOURSELF WALKING THROUGH A HOT AND DRY desert. You've lost your way, and you are extremely thirsty. You're going to need food and water soon, but you have no idea where you're going to find it. You know you can't live much longer under these conditions, and you begin crying out to God for help.

Suddenly, a beautiful staircase that reaches into heaven appears before you. On this staircase is water, food, and everything that pertains to life, for this staircase takes you right into the very presence of God. What an opportunity that would be! Who in their right mind would not take that pathway of deliverance provided by God Himself?

Well, that's exactly what God has done for every one of us. Everyone on earth is walking through this fallen world of sin and death in the deep depravity and weakness of our human nature. Without God's help, there would be no hope, and there would only be certain death and destruction in our future.

Yet God has made a Staircase that will take us immediately out of the bondage of this fallen world and straight into a perfect relationship with Himself. He did not leave us here helpless and alone. No, He provided a pathway of deliverance and revealed that path as a Staircase that reaches into heaven.

In Genesis 28, God revealed this Staircase to Jacob in a dream.

> "Then he dreamed, and behold, a ladder was set
> up on the earth, and its top reached to
> heaven; and there the angels of God were
> ascending and descending on it." (Genesis
> 28:12 NKJV)

The Hebrew word cullam is translated ladder. In other words, it is a staircase (Strong's Concordance #5551). So, Jacob dreamed of a ladder or staircase that reached heaven, and he saw the angels of God *ascending and descending* upon that Staircase.

Years later, in the first chapter of the book of John, Jesus made a reference back to the Staircase that Jacob saw in the dream. Jesus said to Nathaniel,

> "...hereafter you shall see heaven open, and the
> angels of God ascending and descending
> upon the Son of Man." (John 1:51 NKJV)

Notice how Jesus used the same terminology as in Genesis 28:12 when He spoke of the angels *ascending and descending.* Yet instead of speaking of a staircase, Jesus spoke of Himself when he said that the angels of God would ascend and descend upon *the Son of Man.*

Jesus revealed that He, Himself, is the Staircase that Jacob saw in the dream. He is the only way to Heaven, the only path to the Father. Just as He declared in John 14:6,

> "...I am the way, the truth, and the life. No one comes to the Father except through Me."
> (NKJV)

This staircase that Jacob saw in the dream, was one of the primary symbols that God used to represent Jesus in the Old Testament. It is interesting to note, that out of all the examples from the Old Testament that Jesus could have chosen to use when speaking to Nathaniel, Jesus picked this symbol of the staircase to identify Himself as the pathway to the Father.

It is no wonder that God would use a staircase to represent His Son because a staircase simply tells the gospel of Jesus so beautifully. You see, every person had been separated from God through sin, which in turn brought forth death, and so there was a huge gap of sin and death that kept us from fellowship with God. Then God sent His Son Jesus to be the Staircase that would bridge the gap between God and man, thereby providing a great pathway of deliverance back to the Father for all who choose to believe.

THE OLD TESTAMENT WAS THE BLUEPRINT OF THE STAIRCASE

When a builder sets out to build a house, he doesn't just start pouring concrete and putting boards together at random. No, the builder knows that he first needs to draw the plans for the house, which are called the blueprint. The blueprint of a home shows what the house will look like before it is built. After the builder has the blueprint, it is then that he goes to build the house.

That is precisely what God did with the Old Testament. The Old Testament was like a blueprint of the staircase that Jacob dreamed about, and Jesus is that Staircase. God used the Old Testament to show us what the Staircase would look like before He came.

Throughout the Old Testament, and ever since the world was created, God foretold of His Son through prophecies and types and shadows that were given to His chosen people Israel, so that when Jesus came to this earth in the flesh, we would know that He is the Son of God. He chose to identify His Son to us by telling the end from the beginning, as it is written,

> "Remember the former things of old, for I am
> God, and there is no other; I am God, and
> there is none like Me, declaring the end from
> the beginning, and from ancient times things
> that are not yet done, saying, My counsel shall
> stand, and I will do all My pleasure." (Isaiah
> 46:9-10 NKJV)

Only God can tell the end from the beginning, and that is the way He chose to identify His Son to us. All through the Old Testament, God gave witness of His Son before He came to earth so that when He came, we would know that Jesus is the Staircase, the only way to the Father.

TYPES AND SHADOWS

The Old Testament is full of prophecies that God spoke to us in advance, and then they were all fulfilled by one man, Jesus Christ. God not only gave us direct prophecies that were fulfilled by Jesus, such as where He would be born, how He would suffer for our sins, and how He would rise from the grave, but God's testimony of His Son also came in the form of types and shadows throughout the Old Testament. These types and shadows consisted of people, events, numbers, patterns, and symbols, and every one of them told the exact same message, that the Messiah and Savior was coming to deliver us!

Why are these prophecies called types and shadows? The word "type" declares that in His power, God was able to use a person or event in history to be a "like figure" of what Jesus would accomplish. For example, the New Testament described the flood and Noah's Ark as the like figure of baptism in Christ (1st Peter 3:19-22 KJV). This is just one example of how an event that happened in the Old Testament was used as a type and shadow to tell us of Jesus and what He would accomplish.

What is meant by "shadow?" A man once described it to me this way. Let's say that you are standing around a corner of a building, and you see the shadow of a person approaching. As the person continues getting closer, the shadow becomes more and more defined. Then suddenly, the actual person turns the corner, and you can see exactly who that person really is.

Think about that, before the person turned the corner, all you could see was his shadow, but you could not see his actual image. The shadow gave you an idea of what the approaching person would look like, and it also told you that the person was getting closer, but you could not see exactly who the person was until he turned the corner.

That is precisely how God used the entire Old Testament. God used types and shadows, which consisted of people, events, numbers, patterns, and symbols, to proclaim that Jesus was coming to save us. All through the Old Testament, the shadow became more and more defined, and then Jesus turned the corner (when He was born in that manger), and we could see that He is the Son of God, our Messiah and Savior, that God had been speaking of from the very beginning.

In this way, the Old Testament was a blueprint of the Staircase. Whether it was Noah's Ark, Moses, the Red Sea, the 7 days of creation, or the pattern of the Tabernacle, God used the types and shadows of the Old Testament to come together into one magnificent, precise picture of His Son. You've heard it said that a picture is worth a thousand words. Well, every type and shadow in the Bible also speaks a thousand words about the Savior who was coming to bridge the gap between God and man.

The entire Old Testament was all about Him and all that He would accomplish and fulfill. If you were to list all the prophecies, types, and shadows of the Old Testament, they would look like one big picture of a staircase that leads to Heaven, and that Staircase is simply Jesus Himself.

ILLUSTRATION OF THE STAIRCASE

To illustrate the blueprint of the Staircase, you could draw some simple stair steps on a piece of paper and then begin to label each of those steps with one of the significant events of the Old Testament. Then you could look at the staircase you've drawn, and when you see the steps labeled with people like Abraham, Moses, and David, it's easy to see that it was all about Jesus. Every step of that staircase was part of a greater picture that God was revealing.

Here is a simple drawing of the Staircase. Every single prophecy and type and shadow of the Bible would be another step on this Staircase, but I've just chosen eight steps to simplify the illustration.

"The Staircase"

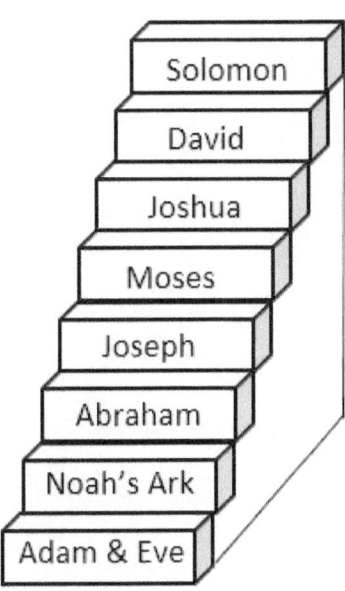

Each one of these steps on the staircase represents a type and shadow of Jesus, demonstrating that He is the only way to get from the fallen world back to the Father. In looking at this staircase, it is easy to see that the entire Old Testament was a blueprint of the staircase that Jacob dreamed about, and that Jesus is that Staircase. Now, let's take a closer look at each of these steps to see how they describe and foretell Jesus.

CHAPTER 2

THE STEPS OF THE STAIRCASE

FIRST STEP- ADAM AND EVE

In the illustration of the staircase, I've labeled the first step of the staircase, "Adam and Eve." From the beginning, from the time of the very first man and woman, God was already speaking to us about His Son.

In Ephesians 5:25-32, Paul revealed a great mystery to us. He was speaking of husbands and wives, and he referred back to the very first husband and wife, Adam and Eve. Then He explained,

> "This is a great mystery, but I speak concerning Christ and the church." (Ephesians 5:32 NKJV)

Paul was letting us in on the mystery of how God used Adam and Eve to be a type and shadow of Jesus and the Church (His bride).

Even the way that Eve was made from Adam's rib (while He was asleep) was a magnificent sign of Christ and the Church. The rib was taken from Adam's side. You'll remember that when Jesus was on the cross, a soldier pierced His side with a spear, and blood and water came out. This blood and water from His side declared the way that the Church was created, for the Church was created through the blood of Jesus and the washing of regeneration through the Holy Spirit (Titus 3:5-7 NKJV).

Therefore, just as Eve was made from a rib taken from Adam's side when he was asleep, so the Church was made from Jesus through His death on the cross. You can see from the beginning, through the first man and woman that He created, God was already foretelling His plan of what Jesus would come to accomplish. He was giving us the blueprint of the Staircase.

SECOND STEP- NOAH'S ARK

I've labeled the second step "Noah's Ark." Many years passed from the time of Adam to Noah. In the days of Noah, it came to pass that the wickedness of man was great in the earth. So, the Lord said that He would destroy man from the face of the earth. Yet Noah found grace in the eyes of the Lord, and God made a way of deliverance for Noah and his family through the ark.

It came to pass that through forty days and nights of rain, eight people on the ark, and the animals on the ark, God started the whole world over because of sin and wickedness. The New Testament tells us that this was "the like figure" of baptism in Christ (1st Peter 3:21 KJV).

The message of this type and shadow is clear. Just as God started the whole world over through the flood and Noah's Ark, we can also start over through Jesus. When a person is baptized in Christ, the waters of baptism declare and display how we are buried with Him in baptism and raised up with Him to new life. Just as 2nd Corinthians 5:17 says,

"Therefore, if anyone is in Christ, he is a new
creation; old things have passed away; behold,
all things are become new." (NKJV)

So, in the account of Noah's Ark, God was foretelling all that Jesus would fulfill and accomplish.

It was all about Jesus...

THIRD STEP- ABRAHAM AND ISAAC

On the third step, we come to "Abraham and Isaac." Many years after Noah's Ark, it came to pass that God chose to give His promise of blessing to Abraham and his son Isaac. Now Isaac was the son who was born through a miracle of God (because his mother, Sarah, was past the age of childbearing when he was conceived). Then, it so happened that God told Abraham to offer his son Isaac as a sacrifice. Abraham obeyed God, but as he took the knife in his hand, the angel of the Lord stopped him. Then God provided His own sacrifice, which was a ram caught in a thicket by its horns.

This all served as a symbol of the greater picture. God's instruction to Abraham to sacrifice his son was actually a testimony of how He Himself, God the Father, would send His own Son Jesus (who was born through a miracle birth) to be the sacrifice for the sins of the world. God was giving us a type and shadow of what He, Himself, would do.

The Bible also records that Abraham believed that God would raise his son Isaac from the dead. As it is written,

> "By faith Abraham, when he was tested, offered
> up Isaac, and he who had received the
> promises offered up his only begotten son, of
> whom it was said, 'in Isaac your seed shall be
> called,' concluding that God was able to raise
> him up, even from the dead, from which he
> also received him in a figurative sense."
> (Hebrews 11:17-19 NKJV)

Just as Abraham believed for Isaac to be raised from the dead, so also God the Father believed for Jesus to be raised. For when the Father sent Jesus to die for our sins, He knew that He would raise Him from the dead. Therefore, God's command to Abraham to sacrifice his son Isaac served as a symbol of the greater picture of all that He Himself would fulfill and accomplish for our sake.

FOURTH STEP- JOSEPH

On the fourth step, we come to Joseph. You'll remember that Abraham begat Isaac, Isaac begat Jacob, and Jacob begat twelve sons. God changed Jacob's name to Israel, and his twelve sons became known as the twelve tribes of Israel.

Joseph was the favored one of Jacob's twelve sons. Through his brothers' evil intentions, he was sold as a slave. Yet God worked their evil for good and raised Joseph to second in command over all of Egypt. By raising Joseph to second in command, God brought provision to Israel through the hand of Joseph.

This all served as a symbol of the greater picture. Just as God used Joseph to save his entire family, so God sent His Son Jesus to save the entire world by paying the price for our sins, and then He rose from the grave to "second in command" at the right hand of the Father. As it is written,

> "But this Man, after He had offered one sacrifice for sins forever, sat down at the right hand of God..." (Hebrews 10:12 NKJV)

Therefore, just as God made provision for Israel through Joseph, God made provision for the world through Jesus.

Also, God had given Joseph two dreams, and in those two dreams, God showed Joseph that his brothers would bow to him. The Bible records that Joseph's brothers did, in fact, bow to him,

> "So Judah and his brothers came to Joseph's house, and he was still there; and they fell before him on the ground." (Genesis 44:14 NKJV)

Just as Joseph's brothers bowed to him, so also, Jesus is now at the right hand of the Father, and the Bible says,

> "Therefore God also has highly exalted Him and given Him the name which is above every

name, that at the name of Jesus every knee
should bow, of those in heaven, and of those
on earth, and of those under the earth, and
that every tongue should confess that Jesus
Christ is Lord, to the glory of God the
Father." (Philippians 2:9-11 NKJV)

It was all about Jesus...

FIFTH STEP-MOSES

On the fifth step, we come to Moses. After Joseph died, another
Pharaoh came that did not know Joseph and brought Israel into
bondage. Several times in the Bible, Egypt is called *the house of
bondage.* God called Moses from a burning bush and sent him to
deliver the Children of Israel, and in doing this, Moses served as a
symbol of the greater picture.

In Hebrews 3:5, The New Testament says that Moses was "...
a testimony of those things which would be spoken afterward..."
(NKJV). So, Moses was a testimony of all that Jesus would fulfill
and accomplish. Just as God sent Moses to deliver Israel out of
the bondage of Egypt, God sent Jesus to deliver us out of the
bondage of sin and this world.

At Mount Sinai (also called Horeb), after God had delivered
the Children of Israel out of Egypt through Moses, the Lord
descended upon the mountain in fire. When they saw the fire
and heard His voice, they asked for Moses to be their intercessor.
God was pleased with the words of the assembly when they
asked for Moses to be their intercessor because they were
beginning to understand the immense gap between God and

man because of sin, and they knew that they needed an intercessor.

Later, Moses would prophesy of Jesus and tell them that there would be a prophet coming like himself according to the words they had spoken in the mount about needing an intercessor and that this prophet, they would have to hear (Deuteronomy 18:15-19; Acts 7:37). Moses was telling them that just as they had learned how they needed an intercessor that day at Mount Sinai, that, in fact, the true Intercessor and Savior was on His way.

MOSES AND THE BURNING BUSH

The burning bush that God used when calling Moses, was also a foreshadowing of Jesus. The Bible says that Moses turned aside to see why the bush was on fire but not consumed (Exodus 3:2-4).

Several times in the Old Testament, Jesus is called the *Branch.* You see, that burning bush represented Jesus. He is the only man (the Branch) who could receive the fire of the Holy Spirit and live. Then He paid the price for us so that we also could receive the fire of the Holy Spirit and live for God. In other words, all who have been cleansed by the blood of Jesus can receive the promise of the Holy Spirit, and instead of being consumed by the fire, are sanctified and brought into perfect fellowship with the Father.

Just as it was on the day of Pentecost, when the disciples were filled with the Holy Spirit, the Bible says,

> "Then there appeared to them divided tongues, as
> of fire, and one sat upon each of them." (Acts
> 2:3 NKJV)

So it was that even in the call to Moses from the burning bush, the Lord was already revealing His plan of redemption through Christ. God was declaring that just as He had sent Moses to deliver Israel out of the bondage of Egypt, so He would one day send Jesus to deliver us out of the bondage of sin and this world so that we could receive the Holy Spirit.

It was all about Jesus...

SIXTH STEP- JOSHUA

After Moses died, God raised up Joshua to lead the people across the Jordan and into the Promised Land. The Bible directly associates the Promised Land with "His Rest." Yet, the New Testament records that when Joshua brought them into the Promised Land, this was not the ultimate fulfillment of God's Rest:

> "For if Joshua had given them rest, then He
>   would not afterward have spoken of another
>   day. There remains therefore a rest for the
>   people of God." (Hebrews 4:8-9 NKJV)

In stating this, God was revealing that the true Rest would only come from the Messiah, Jesus Christ, who would reconcile us to the Father so that we could worship Him in "spirit and truth" (John 4:20-24). Therefore, when Joshua brought the Children of Israel into the Promised Land, this all served as a symbol of the greater picture of how Jesus would be the one who would bring us into the true "Promised Land Rest" of God.

SEVENTH STEP- DAVID

On the seventh step, we come to David. After the death of Joshua, the nation of Israel went through a period in which God raised up judges in the land to deliver His people. Then in the days of Samuel the prophet, the Children of Israel desired to have a King over them. Saul was chosen as the first King of Israel, but he displeased God with his disobedience.

In 1st Samuel 13:14, Samuel gave the message to King Saul that another would be taking his place and that it would be *a man after God's own heart.* Then God raised up David to be the second king of His people Israel. David was Israel's beloved King, and he symbolized the greater picture of how God would send His Son Jesus to be the *"KING OF KINGS AND LORD OF LORDS"* who reigns forevermore (Revelation 19:16 NKJV).

God also gave testimony of how David would be the direct lineage through which Jesus would be born when He said,

> :...I will set up your seed after you, who will be of
> your sons; and I will establish his kingdom.
> He shall build Me a house, and I will establish
> his throne forever. I will be his Father, and he
> shall be My son; and I will not take My mercy
> away from him, as I took it from him who
> was before you. And I will establish him in
> My house and in My Kingdom forever; and
> his throne shall be established forever." (1st
> Chronicles 17:11-14 NKJV)

So, David was not only a type and shadow of the true King,

Jesus Christ, who was to come, but He was also the direct lineage in the flesh through which Jesus Christ would be born.

EIGHTH STEP- SOLOMON

On the eighth step, we come to "Solomon," who was the son of David that built the Temple of God. Now, up until the time of Solomon, the Ark of the Covenant had dwelt in a temporary dwelling made of curtains called the Tabernacle of Moses. King David desired to build a permanent house for God. Yet, through the prophet Nathan, God revealed to David that it would not be himself, but his son that would build the permanent house for God (2nd Samuel 7:12-13).

This is where a revelation of Jesus is found. When God spoke to David about his son who would build the temple, he was, in fact, speaking to David about Jesus. Though Solomon was the son of David, who built the temple, Solomon served as a symbol of the greater picture of how Jesus would come to be the "true Temple." For Jesus is the only man that could receive the Holy Spirit and be the permanent dwelling place of God.

You'll remember that when Jesus walked this earth, He looked over at the temple that Solomon had made and said,

> "...Destroy this temple, and in three days I will
> raise it up." (John 2:19 NKJV)

Yet they did not understand that He was speaking of the temple of His body. Jesus was explaining to them that it was not Solomon's Temple, but He, Himself, who was the true Temple (dwelling place) of God.

This is precisely what Stephen was explaining to the council in Acts Chapter 7, just before they stoned him. As Stephen stood before the council, he led them through the scriptures, starting with Abraham, and going all the way to Solomon, telling them how it was all about Jesus. When he got to Solomon, he explained how Solomon built a house for God, but then he said these words:

> "However, the Most High does not dwell in
> temples made with hands..." (Acts7:48
> NKJV)

Stephen was explaining that God does not dwell in man-made temples but that He dwells in His Son, Jesus. He was telling them that Solomon's temple was a type and shadow of the Son of God, Jesus Christ, the only man that could receive the Holy Spirit.

You see, Jesus is God's permanent dwelling place that David had longed for. Then Jesus paid the price for our sins so that we, too, could receive the precious gift of the Holy Spirit and live for God.

EVERY STEP DECLARES HIM

Therefore, the entire Old Testament is a blueprint of the Staircase, and every single step of the Staircase foretold of Jesus. Through Adam and Eve, God spoke of Jesus and the Church (His bride). Through Noah, God showed us how we could start over fresh and new in Christ. Through Abraham, God declared that He, the Father, would send His only begotten Son (by way of a miracle birth) to be the sacrifice for the world, and that He would raise Him from the grave.

Through Joseph, God spoke of how Jesus would be raised to second in command at the Father's right hand, thereby making provision for the whole world. Through Moses, God was telling us that Jesus would deliver us from the bondage of sin and this world so that we could receive the Holy Spirit and not be consumed. Through Joshua, God foretold of the true Promised Land Rest that would be given to us through Jesus.

Through David, God gave us a foreshadowing of *the King of Kings and Lord of Lords,* Jesus Christ, who reigns forevermore. And through Solomon (the son of David who built the temple), God gave us a picture of the true Temple, Jesus Christ, the only man who could receive the Holy Spirit, and who would then pay the price for our sins so that we too could receive the precious gift of the Holy Spirit. It was all about Jesus.

In the illustration of the Staircase, I used only eight types and shadows. Still, every prophecy and every type and shadow of the Old Testament is simply another step on this Staircase that represents Jesus. Through this Staircase, God was telling us that all have sinned and fallen short of the glory of God and that Jesus is the only way to cross that gap and get back into His Presence.

The entire Old Testament is like one big portrait of a beautiful Staircase, hand-painted by God, and it is His loving invitation for all to take the pathway of deliverance that He has provided. He is waiting for each one of us to simply say yes to Jesus.

CHAPTER 3

THE FIRST ADAM AND THE LAST ADAM

As we walk up the steps of this amazing Staircase, God is constantly letting us in on a little more of the mystery of Christ (Colossians 2:2). He unveiled it to us step by step, here a little, and there a little, as it is written in Isaiah 28:10,

> "For precept must be upon precept, precept upon
> precept, line upon line, line upon line, here a
> little, there a little." (NKJV)

Throughout the Old Testament, as God was painting the picture of this beautiful staircase, the message of the gospel was hidden until Jesus came and fulfilled it all. Now let's go back to the beginning when God had made everything perfect in the garden of Eden, as we look further into how God used the first man Adam to be a type and shadow of the Savior who was to come.

THE PERFECT GARDEN

It was a beautiful day in the Garden of Eden. Adam and his wife (whom he would later name Eve) walked in the light of God's Rest and perfection as they were in perfect fellowship with God. There was no pain, no suffering, no sickness, and no sorrow. They enjoyed all the glorious splendor of God's creation as they beheld the greatness of His wondrous works.

There was so much to do and so many things to explore and see. They could eat from any tree in the garden, even the Tree of Life, yet there was only one thing that the Lord had told Adam not to do. The Lord had told Adam not to eat from the Tree of the Knowledge of Good and Evil, and He warned him that on the day that he ate from this tree, he would surely die.

It came to pass, on this particular day, that the serpent deceived the woman by twisting God's Word and causing her to believe and act upon a lie. Instead of seeing the truth about this Tree of the Knowledge of Good and Evil, how that eating from it would cause her to die, the serpent, with all his craft and subtlety, influenced the woman so that she began to see the tree differently. Instead of seeing the tree as something to stay away from, she began to see the tree as something good for food, pleasant to the eyes, and as something desirable to make her wise (Genesis 3:6).

The serpent had taken God's truth and turned it into a lie. The woman believed the serpent's lie more than God's truth, and she took from the tree and ate, and then gave it to her husband Adam, who also ate from the tree. Immediately they died a spiritual death in that they were separated from God, and they knew that they were naked. Though their flesh did not die for many years to come, they died a spiritual death that very day, for they were separated from God because of sin.

And so, Adam and his wife were made to leave the perfect garden the Lord had made for them. Sin and death had now entered the creation, and so the whole creation was separated from God's Rest, and it became the fallen world. There was now a gap (or breach) between God and His creation because of sin.

THE PROMISED SEED

Yet before Adam and Eve had ever left the garden of Eden, God foretold of the coming of the "Seed" of the woman that would bruise the serpent's head (Genesis 3:15). From the very beginning, God foretold of the coming of this Seed, the Messiah and Savior, who would deliver us from the sin and death that had separated us from God.

In the New Testament, the Bible reveals that this Seed is Jesus Christ,

> "Now to Abraham and his Seed were the
> promises made. He does not say, 'And to
> seeds,' as of many, but as of one, 'And to your
> Seed,' who is Christ." (Galatians 3:16 NKJV)

The promise of blessing had been given to Abraham and his *"Seed,"* and so the Bible reveals that Jesus is the Seed to whom the promise of blessing was made.

It was this very same Seed who was spoken of in the garden of Eden, and it was this Seed that would be the Staircase which would bring us out of the bondage of this world and back into the rest and presence of God. All down through the ages, ever since sin and death entered into the creation, man has looked for and waited for this Seed, this deliverer, who would come and bring us back to the Father.

THE SEED IS THE LAST ADAM, THE SECOND MAN

Therefore, it was the first man Adam who failed and brought the world into the curse, darkness, sin, and death. Yet it was the Seed, Jesus Christ, that would come to deliver us from all the bondage that was brought on by the first Adam.

In Romans 5:14, the Bible makes it clear that the first man (Adam) was a type, or like figure, of Him who was to come, Jesus Christ. Also, the Bible specifically calls Jesus "the last Adam" and "the second Man." 1st Corinthians 15:45-47 says,

> "And so it is written, The first man Adam became a living being. The last Adam became a life-giving spirit. However, the spiritual is not first, but the natural, and afterward, the spiritual. The first man was of the earth, made of dust; the second Man is the Lord from heaven." (NKJV)

So, the Bible clearly refers to Jesus as *the last Adam* and *the second Man.*

It was the first Adam that failed and brought sin and death into the world, and it was the last Adam or second Man, Jesus Christ, who came to this earth and won the victory over sin and death by which He gave every man the opportunity to be saved. In Romans 5:19, Paul described it this way,

> "For as by one man's disobedience many were
> made sinners, so also by one Man's obedience
> many will be made righteous." (NKJV)

Paul was describing how God made everything perfect in the beginning, and then the whole creation was brought into bondage through the first Adam. Then God sent His Son Jesus Christ (the last Adam) to defeat sin and death, thereby giving every person the opportunity to be delivered from bondage by being born again.

In Romans chapter 8, Paul explains what it means to be born again. He said that when we receive Jesus as our Savior,

> "The Spirit Himself bears witness with our spirit
> that we are children of God..." (Romans 8:16
> NKJV)

You see, before Jesus came and saved us, His Spirit was not bearing witness with our spirit, because we were spiritually dead and filled with sin. Now that Jesus has come and paid the price for our sins, we all have the opportunity to believe and be born again, and it is then that the light of God will shine in our hearts through Jesus when the Holy Spirit comes in (2nd Corinthians 4:6-7).

THE LAST ADAM BROUGHT THE BLESSING

It is very important to understand that the first Adam lived in a perfect world, and he was disobedient by the one thing he was told not to do, and thereby brought the curse, darkness, sin, and death upon all. Yet Jesus came into a fallen world full of sin and death all around him, and overcame it all, thereby bringing the blessing upon all who will believe.

When Jesus was born into this fallen world, He came right into Satan's territory. He came into the domain of "the prince of the power of the air" (Ephesians 2:2), and disarmed him of all power (Colossians 2:15). Sin was condemning us, and then Jesus condemned sin in the flesh. As it is written in Romans 8:3,

> "...God sending his own Son in the likeness of
> sinful flesh, and for sin, condemned sin in the
> flesh." (KJV)

Jesus came into this sinful world and lived a perfect life. Then He gave His perfect life for us and rose from the grave so we could receive the promise of blessing. And so, it was the first Adam who sinned and brought the curse, and it was the last Adam, Jesus Christ, who paid the price for the curse so that we could receive the blessing, which is the Holy Spirit.

. . .

THE PROMISE OF BLESSING IS THE PROMISE OF THE HOLY SPIRIT

THE NEW TESTAMENT REVEALS THAT THE PROMISE OF blessing given to Abraham and his Seed (Jesus Christ) is the promise of the Holy Spirit. As it is written in Galatians 3:13-14,

> "Christ has redeemed us from the curse of the
> law, having become a curse for us (for it is
> written, 'Cursed is everyone who hangs on a
> tree'), that the blessing of Abraham might
> come upon the Gentiles in Christ Jesus, that
> we might receive the promise of the Spirit
> through faith." (NKJV)

So, the Bible tells us that the blessing of Abraham (that now comes upon the Gentiles through Jesus Christ) is the promise of the Holy Spirit. It was the first Adam that brought the curse, and it was the last Adam, Jesus Christ, who gave us the blessing which is the Holy Spirit.

A CONSTANT THEME

Throughout His Word, God gave us the constant theme and message of "the first Adam and the last Adam." Through this message, God clearly establishes that it was the first man (Adam) that failed, and it was the last Adam or second Man, Jesus Christ, who prevailed and won the victory over sin and death.

This "last Adam, or second Man," is the Seed that was spoken of from the beginning, and that Seed is the Staircase that would bring us out of the bondage of the world and back into the presence of God by giving us the Holy Spirit. From the beginning, God was bringing the Staircase into clearer view, step by step, here a little and there a little, so that when Jesus came in the flesh, we would know that He is the Staircase that the Father had been painting the portrait of all along.

CHAPTER 4

THE PATTERN OF SECONDS

WE HAVE BEEN LOOKING AT THE MESSAGE OF THE FIRST Adam, that failed, and the last Adam, Jesus Christ, who prevailed over sin and death. God not only gave us the message of "the first Adam and the last Adam," but He also confirmed this message with a specific pattern that you can find over and over in the Bible. I will refer to this pattern as the "Pattern of Seconds."

The Pattern of Seconds always declares that it was not the "first," but the "second" that God blessed. By displaying that His blessing is on the "second," God foretold that His blessing would not be on the first man (Adam) who failed, but on the second Man, the last Adam, Jesus Christ, who won the victory. In other words, in this pattern, it was always the "second" that represented Jesus and foretold of the Seed who was to come, the Staircase that leads to heaven.

There are many examples of this pattern throughout God's Word, and each one is like a connecting thread that constantly confirms and displays God's foreknowledge and power to foretell the coming of the Seed that was spoken of in the garden. Just as God declares that only He can tell the end from the beginning, this Pattern of Seconds was used all through the ages to declare the gospel of Jesus, so that when He came to this earth to save us, we would know that this is indeed the Messiah and Savior that God had been speaking of from the beginning.

Now let's look at this pattern and follow it through the Bible. As you read through these examples, remember that each one declares the message of how it was the first Adam that failed, and it was the last Adam, the second Man, Jesus Christ, who prevailed and won the victory. There are many more examples, but here is a list of ten.

Example 1: Cain and Abel

Cain was the firstborn son of Adam, and Abel was his second-born. It was not Cain (the firstborn), but Abel (the second-born) who brought the pleasing sacrifice to God. Cain killed his brother Abel, and the Bible makes it clear that the death of this righteous man was a direct foreshadowing of Jesus and all that He would accomplish at the cross.

Hebrews 12:24 says that the blood of Jesus speaks "better things than that of Abel." So, it was the second-born that God used to declare Jesus, whom the Bible calls the last Adam and the second Man.

Example 2: Ishmael and Isaac

Ishmael was Abraham's firstborn son, born through Sarah's handmaid, Hagar. Isaac was Abraham's second-born son, and he was born through Sarah. It was not Ishmael (his firstborn), but Isaac (his second-born) to whom the promises were made.

Isaac (his second-born) was also the one that represented Jesus when God told Abraham to sacrifice his son. Here again, God used the "second" to represent Jesus, and to confirm the message of how the blessing is not given to those who are of the first Adam that failed, but to those who are of the last Adam, or second Man, Jesus Christ who prevailed.

Example 3: Esau and Jacob

Isaac and Rebekah had twins, and their names were Esau and Jacob. Even while these twins were still in the womb, God told Rebekah that, "...the older shall serve the younger" (Genesis 25:23 NKJV). And so it came to pass that it was not Esau (the older twin), but Jacob (the younger twin or second-born) who received the blessing from his father, Isaac.

Jacob (the second-born) was also the one whose name was later changed to Israel. He is the one who received the same promises that God had given to his grandfather Abraham and his father Isaac, and he was also the lineage through whom Christ came. Here again, it was the "second" born that received the blessing, and that which God used as a type and shadow of the last Adam, the second Man, Jesus Christ.

Example 4: Manasseh and Ephraim

Joseph was the eleventh son of Jacob, and he was sold into slavery in Egypt. While in Egypt, he had two sons, and their names were Manasseh and Ephraim. It was not Manasseh (the firstborn), but Ephraim (the second-born) that Jacob purposely gave the blessing to by crossing his hands and placing his right hand upon him (Genesis 48:8-20).

By doing this, he continued the same pattern of blessing in

that the blessing was given to the second-born. God was constantly telling us about Jesus, the second Man, who would come and receive the blessing, which is the promise of the Holy Spirit.

Example 5: Zerah and Perez

Judah was the fourth son of Jacob, and he was the direct lineage through whom Jesus would come in the flesh. Judah had twins named Zerah and Perez. Zerah was in the process of being born first and was declared to be the firstborn. The Bible says that Zerah,

" ...put out his hand; and the midwife took a scarlet thread and bound it on his hand, saying, 'This one came out first.' Then it happened, as he drew back his hand, that his brother came out unexpectedly; and she said, 'How did you break through? This breach be upon you!' Therefore his name was called Perez" (Genesis 38:28-29 NKJV).

So Zerah (the one with the scarlet thread) was declared the firstborn, but then Perez broke forth and took his place, and the midwife proclaimed that this "breach" would be upon him. It is necessary to understand a couple of terms here. A breach is used to describe the gap between God and man, which was caused by Adam's sin. Also, scarlet is used to represent our sins. Just as Isaiah 1:18 says, "...though your sins are like scarlet, they shall be as white as snow..." (NKJV).

Just as Perez was the second-born, who broke forth to take the place of Zerah (who was declared to be the firstborn with the scarlet thread), so also, God was telling us that the last Adam, or second Man, Jesus Christ, would "break forth" to take the sins of the first Adam upon Himself.

God was telling us that Jesus would take the breach (that was caused by our sins) upon Himself. As Jesus was on the cross, He was there in our place. He took our "scarlet" sins upon Himself, and made us white as snow, and He became the restorer of the breach between God and man.

So, in the account of Zerah and Perez, God was telling us the gospel of Jesus, and how it would be the "second" man that would break forth to deliver us. Also, in further confirmation of how Perez (the second-born) represented Jesus in this type and shadow, Matthew 1:3 states that Perez was of the direct lineage of Jesus Christ.

Example 6: First and Second Set of Stone Tablets

God gave Moses the Ten Commandments on tablets of stone at two different times because the first set was broken. The first time that Moses brought the Ten Commandments down from the mountain, he broke the tablets because of Israel's disobedience. The second time he brought the Ten Commandments down (on the second set of tablets), He placed them in the Ark of the Covenant, which was covered by the Mercy Seat.

The first set of tablets that were broken represent how the first Adam, along with everyone born of the flesh, could not keep the law of God. The second set of tablets, which were placed in the Ark under the Mercy Seat, declare that it was the last Adam, or second Man, Jesus Christ, that would fulfill the law and give mercy to all who call upon Him.

In other words, with this second set of tablets being placed in the Ark of the Covenant, God was foretelling that the only way the Ten Commandments could be satisfied and fulfilled was through the mercy of His Son Jesus, the last Adam, the second Man.

Example 7: First and Second Generation

After Israel was delivered from the bondage of Egypt, it was not the first generation, but the second generation that entered the Promised Land. The first generation represents the first Adam who failed, and the second generation represents the last Adam, the second Man, Jesus Christ, who entered the Rest of God for us. Here again, God used the Pattern of Seconds to represent Jesus.

Example 8: Entrance into the Promised Land

God chose Joshua from the tribe of Ephraim to bring Israel into the Promised Land. Ephraim was the second-born of Joseph, who had received the blessing from Jacob. So, when God chose Joshua to bring His people into the Promised Land, He was choosing one who was of the lineage of the second-born to bring them across the Jordan.

In doing this, God was keeping with the same Pattern of Seconds, which served as a symbol of the greater picture of how Jesus, the last Adam, the second Man, would bring us into the true Promised Land Rest of God.

Example 9: First King & the Second King

Saul was the first King of Israel. He displeased God with his disobedience, so God replaced him with another. So, the first King (Saul) was used to represent the first Adam that failed, and it was the second King (David), the man after God's own heart, who was used to represent the last Adam, the second Man, Jesus Christ, who prevailed.

This second King was also the one who was the direct lineage through which Jesus would come. So, God even used the first two Kings of Israel to declare the Pattern of Seconds.

Example 10: First and Second Birth

The first way that each of us is born is in the flesh. Every person born into this world partakes in this first birth. When we are born in the flesh from our mother's womb, we are born into sin in the likeness of the first Adam who failed. Then Jesus came to pay the price for our sins so that every person could have the opportunity to be born again through the Spirit, or you could say, born a second time.

So, it is not in our first birth that we are saved, but it is only through our second birth, when we are born of the Spirit through believing in Jesus, that we are saved. So, the Pattern of Seconds is even found as we are born again in Christ.

The Pattern of Seconds can be found throughout the Old Testament, and it always declares the message of how it was the first Adam that failed and the last Adam, the second Man, Jesus Christ, who prevailed to bring us out of the bondage that was brought on by the first Adam.

THE LAST ADAM IS ALSO THE FIRSTBORN

When studying God's Word concerning the message of "The first Adam and the last Adam" and how the Pattern of Seconds was used to confirm that same message, it is of utmost importance to make a clear distinction that the last Adam or second Man, Jesus Christ, is also the firstborn.

You see, concerning that He came in the flesh, He is the last Adam, the second Man, who humbled Himself to come into this world as a man and pay the price for our sins so that we could be saved. Yet this last Adam, or second Man, also rose from the grave and became the "firstborn" from the dead so that He might have the preeminence in all things.

Not only did He become the firstborn from the dead, but He is also the firstborn or the beginning of the creation of God (Revelation 3:14), for He is before all things, and He is the only begotten Son of God. As it is written of Jesus,

> "He is the image of the invisible God, the
>   firstborn over all creation. For by Him all
>   things were created that are in heaven and
>   that are on earth, visible and invisible,
>   whether thrones or dominions or
>   principalities or powers. All Things were
>   created through Him and for Him. And He is
>   before all things, and in Him all things
>   consist. And He is the head of the body, the
>   church, who is the beginning, the firstborn
>   from the dead, that in all things He may have
>   the preeminence. For it pleased the Father
>   that in Him all the fullness should dwell..."
> (Colossians 1:15-19 NKJV)

Also, as it is written,

> "... Jesus Christ, the faithful witness, the firstborn
> from the dead, and the ruler over the kings of
> the earth. To Him who loved us and washed
> us from our sins in His own blood..."
> (Revelation 1:5 NKJV)

Also, the Bible declares us to be the church, "...of the firstborn..." (Hebrews 12:23 NKJV).

Therefore, both the message of "The first Adam and the last Adam" and the "Pattern of Seconds" have to do with Jesus coming in the flesh, and they both tell the gospel. It is the divine order in which God sent His Son in the flesh to redeem fallen man. Yet this last Adam (the second Man) is also the "firstborn" because He is the beginning of the creation of God, the only begotten Son of God, and the firstborn from the dead that He might have the preeminence in all things.

CHAPTER 5

THE NUMBER "66"

GOD WANTS EVERYONE TO WALK UP THE STEPS OF THIS beautiful Staircase, and it is remarkable to see how God painted a picture of this Staircase from the very beginning of creation and throughout the Bible. It was God's desire that when Jesus came in the flesh, we could have confirmation upon confirmation through His Holy Word that Jesus is the Staircase, the only path to heaven.

We have been looking at the message of "The first Adam and the last Adam" and how this message was foretold and confirmed through the "Pattern of Seconds." For even further confirmation, He also attached a specific number to this message, and that number is the number "66". The number 66 was hidden throughout the Old Testament to declare the same message that He had fashioned from the beginning, how it was the first Adam that failed and the last Adam, Jesus Christ, who prevailed over sin and death.

To understand the meaning of the number 66 and how it is

attached to the message of "The first Adam and the last Adam", we must first find the meaning of the number "6" and understand how we can conclude its meaning in the Bible.

THE NUMBERS OF THE LORD

Throughout the Bible, God chose to use numbers to tell the story of Jesus. He is the one who created numbers, and the Bible even starts by using numbers to declare the seven days of creation. So, numbers are obviously very important to God. The mystery of Christ was hidden in the Old Testament, and one of the ways that God concealed this mystery was in the numbers that He chose to use to tell the gospel of Jesus.

Now that Jesus has come in the flesh and revealed the mystery, we can look at the numbers that God used in the Old Testament and find that God was speaking of Jesus with these numbers through the ages, beginning with the seven days of creation.

FOUNDATION FOR UNDERSTANDING THE NUMBERS OF GOD

As we come upon certain numbers that God chose to use in His Word, we should always ask ourselves, "What does this number mean to God?" If we can find out what a number means to God and why He chose to use it in the way He did, then we can learn more about Him.

In the first book of the Bible, God gives us a foundation for understanding His numbers, and this foundation was based on the seventh day in which God rested from His perfect works.

> "And on the seventh day God ended His work
> which He had done, and He rested on the
> seventh day from all His work which He had
> done." (Genesis 2:2 NKJV)

What does the number 7 mean to God? If you ask any Christian what they believe the number 7 means, most everyone would agree on the same meaning. The number 7 represents God's Rest from His complete and perfect works. In other words, the number 7 stands for God's Rest and completion (or perfection).

Now ask yourself how you came to that conclusion. The answer is very simple. We come to that conclusion by basing it on what God did on the seventh day. Since God rested from His complete and perfect works on the seventh day, the number 7 represents God's Rest and completion (or perfection).

Therefore, the meaning of the number 7 is based on what God did on that particular day of creation. We can follow that same pattern of understanding with the previous six days and find each of their meanings as well. Whatever God did on each day of creation will tell us what each number means to Him. Now, let's find the meaning of the number 6.

"6" IS THE NUMBER OF MAN

What did God do on the sixth day of creation? On the sixth day, God made the beasts of the field and the creeping things, and then He made man in His image, male and female, He created them (Genesis 1:24-31). Now ask yourself, "What was the primary or most important thing God did on the sixth day?" The answer, of course, is that He made man in His image (male and female, He created them).

Now, based on the same pattern of understanding by which we concluded the meaning of the number 7, we can conclude that 6 is the number of "man." Why? Because God made man on the sixth day, and that which He did on each day of creation tells what the number stands for.

APPLY THE MEANING OF THE NUMBER 6 TO SCRIPTURE

Since we know that 6 is the number of man, let's apply this understanding to scripture. In Romans 5:19, Paul writes,

> "For as by one man's disobedience many were
> made sinners, so also by one Man's obedience
> many will be made righteous."

Now apply the number 6 to the word "man" in this scripture because 6 is the number of man.

For as by one man's (6) disobedience many were made sinners, so also by one Man's (6) obedience many will be made righteous.

When you apply the number 6 to the word "man," a hidden revelation can be found. God uses one "6" to represent the first Adam that failed, and a second "6" to represent the last Adam, the second Man, Jesus Christ who won the victory and prevailed. It was through the first man (who is represented by a number 6) that death came, and it was through the second Man (who is represented by another number 6) that life and righteousness came.

When you combine these two numbers, they represent "66." All through the Bible you will find that God uses either "two groups of 6" or the actual number "66" to declare the message of the first man (6), Adam, that failed, and the second Man (6), the last Adam, Jesus Christ who prevailed and won the victory. For the number "66" declares the gospel of Jesus Christ.

HOW MANY BOOKS ARE THERE IN GOD'S WORD?

When you understand what the number 66 means to God, it is easy to understand why God placed exactly "66 books" in the Bible. For even the very number of books that He placed in His Word declare the gospel and the victory of the last Adam, the second Man, Jesus Christ, who prevailed over sin and death.

In His Wisdom, God chose to give us His Word through the hands of men inspired by the Holy Spirit. Just as it is written,

"All scripture is given by inspiration of God..."
(2nd Timothy 3:16 NKJV)

After God went to such great lengths to give His Word to men through the inspiration of the Holy Spirit, and to have them write it down and record it, do we not think that God would also watch over those writings and have them put together in the exact way that He wanted it done? Of course, He did.

In the book of Jeremiah, God declares,

"...You have seen well, for I am ready to perform My word." (Jeremiah 1:12 NKJV)

Now apply that scripture to the entire Word of God (the Bible). God watched over His Word to perform it, and He placed the exact number of books in the Bible that He Himself chose to be there. There are sixty-six books in the Bible because God chose that exact number of books to bring glory to His Son. Just as the Bible says,

"Known unto God are all His works from the
beginning of the world." (Acts 15:18 KJV)

God had the complete plan for the Bible from the beginning. So, of course, He knew that He would write the Bible through the hands of men inspired by the Holy Spirit, and of course, He knew that He would put the sixty-six books of the Bible together through the hands of men, and that this too would be led by the Holy Spirit. His works are always intentional and on purpose.

EXAMPLES OF "66" IN THE BIBLE

Not only did He place this exact number of books in His Word, but He also declared and foretold this exact number throughout the Bible. So that when we read the Bible today, we can know that God foretold of this number 66 long before the sixty-six books of the Bible were put together.

In doing this, He again showed His power to declare the end from the beginning and gave us confirmation that He placed the exact number of books in the Bible that He had already chosen to be there. Now, let's look at examples of the "two groups of 6" and the number "66" hidden in the Old Testament

"66" IN THE PROMISED LAND

God directed the Children of Israel to go to two mountains when they reached the Promised Land (Deuteronomy 27:11-13). He called for six of the tribes to proclaim the blessing at Mount Gerizim, and six of the tribes to proclaim the curse at Mount Ebal.

Do you see the pattern? God divided the tribes into two groups of six. One of the groups of six declared the curse, and one of the groups of six declared the blessing. Just as one man, Adam (represented by the number 6), brought the curse, and one man, Jesus Christ (also represented by the number 6), brought the blessing.

Therefore, when they entered the Promised Land, God gave them a sign of two groups of six (or you could say the number 66), which declared all that Jesus would accomplish and how it would only be through Jesus, the last Adam, the second Man, that we could cross over into the true Promised Land Rest of God.

"66" IN EZEKIEL'S VISION OF THE TEMPLE

God gave Ezekiel a vision of the temple. As Ezekiel described the entrance into the temple, the two groups of six are found again.

> "Afterward he brought me to the temple, and measured the posts, six cubits broad on the one side, and six cubits broad on the other side, which was the breadth of the tabernacle." (Ezekiel 41:1 KJV)

So, the entrance of the temple in Ezekiel's vision measured six cubits on one side, and six cubits on the other.

Here again, we find the two groups of six, or the number "66," which gives the message of the gospel of Jesus, how the first Adam (6) failed, and the last Adam (6), Jesus Christ, prevailed. These two groups of six at the entrance of the temple were God's declaration and testimony that the only way into a relationship with Him was through the precious blood of the last Adam, the second Man, Jesus Christ.

THE TWO ONYX STONES OF THE HIGH PRIEST

This same pattern of two groups of six is also found in the two onyx stones which sat on the shoulders of the High Priest.

> "Then you shall take two onyx stones and engrave
> on them the names of the sons of Israel: six of
> their names on one stone and six names on
> the other stone, in order of their birth....and
> you shall put the two stones on the shoulders
> of the ephod as memorial stones for the sons
> of Israel. So Aaron shall bear their names
> before the Lord on his two shoulders as a
> memorial." (Exodus 28:9-12 NKJV)

Six names were listed on one shoulder and six on the other. Here again, we find the two groups of six, representing the first man Adam who failed, and the last Adam, the second Man, Jesus Christ, who won the victory.

The High Priest in the Old Testament (who wore this ephod

with the two groups of six on his shoulders) was a representation of what Jesus would come to fulfill, for the New Testament declares that Jesus is our High Priest (Hebrews 3:1). The High Priest was the only one who could enter the Holy of Holies in the Tabernacle, and only on the Day of Atonement.

So, when the High Priest in the Old Testament entered beyond the veil into the Holy of Holies, these two groups of six (or the number "66") gave testimony to all that Jesus would bear on His shoulders and accomplish for our sake so that we can now enter that Holy Place (the presence of God) through His blood.

THE TABLE OF SHOWBREAD

The Table of Showbread was one of the articles of furniture in the Tabernacle of Moses. There were twelve loaves of bread on this table, and the Bible describes how they were to be placed. They were instructed to set them in two rows of six.

> "And you shall take fine flour and bake twelve
> cakes with it...You shall set them in two rows,
> six in a row, on the pure gold table before the
> Lord." (Leviticus 24:5-6 NKJV)

Here again, we find the pattern of two groups of six (or the number "66"), which declare the first man (6) that failed, and the second Man (6), Jesus Christ, who prevailed.

This symbol was displayed on the table, and it stood in the area of the Tabernacle that you must go through to get to the Most Holy Place. God was declaring that the only way into the Holy of Holies (Most Holy Place) beyond the veil, was for Jesus (the last Adam, the second Man) to win the victory over sin and death.

11-DAY JOURNEY AND THE NUMBER "66"

Deuteronomy 1:2 specifically points out that there was an "11" day journey from Horeb (Mount Sinai) to Kadesh Barnea. God gave us a specific count of an 11-day journey for a reason. Mount Sinai was where the law was given, and Kadesh Barnea was where they were first told to cross over into the Promised Land. So, God gave us a specific period of days, as was the time it would take (from Mount Sinai) to cross the Wilderness and get to the Promised Land.

This count of eleven days holds a hidden revelation of the number "66." For if you count the consecutive numerals (or integers) of each day, you get the sum of 66. In Mathematics, there is a formula for adding consecutive numbers. In this formula, "n" is the number you are solving for.

n (the first integer + the last integer)/2 = the sum

For Example: 11 (1 + 11) divided by 2 = 66

In simpler terms, you just add each numeral together to reach the sum: **1+2+3+4+5+6+7+8+9+10+11= 66**

Since the 11-day journey holds a hidden revelation of the number 66, and the number 66 declares the gospel of Jesus, God was giving us a revelation that the distance of the journey from Mount Sinai (where the law was given) to the Promised Land could only be fulfilled through Jesus. The only way for us to cross over the Wilderness into the Promised Land Rest was for God to send His Son, Jesus Christ, to pay the price for our sins which were brought on by the first Adam.

JOSEPH WAS THE ELEVENTH SON OF JACOB

As we just saw in the example of the "11-day journey," the number 11 is a hidden revelation of the number "66" when you add up the consecutive numbers one through eleven (1+2+3+4+5+6+7+8+9+10+11= 66). Now apply this revelation of the number 11 to Joseph, Jacob's eleventh son. As we discussed in Chapter Two, Joseph was one of the main types and shadows in the Old Testament that God used to foreshadow Jesus, and his entire life painted a picture of all that Jesus would accomplish for us.

When you understand that the number eleven is actually a hidden revelation of the number 66, it is easy to see why God would use Joseph, who was the eleventh son of Jacob, to be one of the key figures in the Old Testament to represent how Jesus would come to save us. This serves as another revelation of the number "66" that was hidden in God's Word.

TWO GROUPS OF 6 IN JESUS'S FIRST MIRACLE

In the second chapter of the Book of John, the Bible records Jesus's first miracle in which He turned water into wine. Here again, God gave us a sign of the two groups of six, for there were six pots of water, and then there were six pots of wine after Jesus miraculously changed the contents. Here again, the Lord was declaring the first Adam (6) that failed and the last Adam (6) that prevailed.

Jesus said to fill the pots to the brim with water. Just as water was used in the days of Noah's Ark to represent God's judgment, so also, the water in the six pots represented the judgment of the six days of creation that were separated from God's Rest because of the first Adam's sin.

Then Jesus turned the six pots of water into six pots of wine. Just as wine was used in the Lord's supper to represent Jesus's blood, so also the wine in the six pots represented His blood that would be shed at the cross to bring mercy to all who will believe.

So, the six pots of water declared that the First Adam brought judgment upon all, and the six pots of wine declared that the last Adam, the second Man, Jesus Christ, turned judgment into mercy for all who believe. Therefore, in the very first miracle of Jesus, God gave testimony of the two groups of six (or the number 66) to declare the gospel of Jesus.

In all these examples, God was declaring the gospel of Jesus, how the first man (6) failed, and the second Man (6), the last Adam, Jesus Christ, prevailed over sin and death. Knowing the meaning that this number contains, it is no wonder that God would place this exact number of books in the Bible so that even the number of books in His Word would declare the victory of the last Adam, Jesus Christ.

All through the Old Testament, God was declaring this number 66 so that when Jesus came in the flesh, it would be revealed that God's plan was in place from the beginning. Now we will look even further into this number and see how the number 66 was even hidden in the measurements and numbers of the furniture of one of the most significant structures of the Old Testament, the Tabernacle of Moses.

CHAPTER 6

THE HIDDEN NUMBER OF THE TABERNACLE

THE TABERNACLE OF MOSES WAS THE DESIGNATED place of worship that God established among the Children of Israel, and it was one of the primary patterns that God used in the Old Testament to declare the gospel of Jesus. God gave Moses the instructions for the Tabernacle and told him to make everything according to the pattern.

> "And let them make Me a sanctuary, that I may
> dwell among them. According to all that I
> show you, that is, the pattern of the
> tabernacle and the pattern of all its
> furnishings, just so you shall make it."
> (Exodus 25:8-9 NKJV)

Since the number 66 declares the victory of Jesus over sin and death, it is no wonder that this same number can even be found in the measurements and numbers of the furniture of the Tabernacle. The furniture of the Tabernacle consisted of the Altar of Burnt Offering, the Laver, the Table of Showbread, the Menorah, the Altar of Incense, and the Ark of the Covenant.

The Tabernacle

A KEY TO GOD'S SYSTEM OF MEASUREMENTS

When the Lord gives specific measurements and patterns in His Word, we can know that these measurements and patterns must be important to Him and hold very special meaning. They are so important that the Book of Hebrews even calls the Tabernacle and its furnishings the *patterns of heavenly things*. This means that God uses these physical patterns and measurements to help us understand the spiritual elements of the Kingdom of God that we cannot see.

In the book of Ezekiel, there is a key that unlocks the way God wants us to see the measurements that He gives. In Ezekiel 48:30-35, God gave Ezekiel the measurements of the four sides of the wall of the court of the Temple. Ezekiel described that each side of the wall was 4,500 cubits, and then he gave the sum of those four sides, which was 18,000 cubits.

Since the Bible tells us in 2nd Timothy 3:16, "all scripture is given by inspiration of God..." *(NKJV)*, we can know that God had Ezekiel write the sum of those four sides (the perimeter measurement) for a reason. Here we find a key to God's system of measurements. When God gives the measurement of four sides of an object, it is necessary to add the four sides and get the sum.

We can know that the sum of four sides (the perimeter measurement) is important to God because God gave us this example Himself, and by giving us this example, he gave us a foundation for understanding what is important to Him concerning the measurements that He provides.

APPLY THIS SYSTEM OF MEASUREMENT TO THE ARK OF THE COVENANT

Now let's take this same system of measurement (the sum of the four sides) and apply it to the main piece of furniture of the Tabernacle-- the Ark of the Covenant.

In Exodus 25:10, God gives us the measurements of the four sides of the Ark of the Covenant,

"And they shall make an ark of acacia wood; two and a half cubits shall be its length, a cubit and a half its width, and a cubit and a half its height." (NKJV)

Looking at the overhead view, or the perimeter measurement, of the Ark of the Covenant, we have a length of 2 ½ cubits, plus a width of 1 ½ cubits, plus a length of 2 ½ cubits, plus a width of 1 ½ cubits. The sum of all four sides, the perimeter measurement, equals eight cubits.

THE ARK BEARS THE NUMBER 8 IN MEASUREMENT

The Ark of the Covenant (overhead view)-

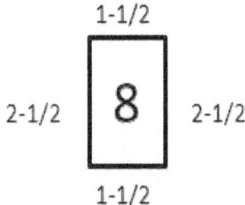

1-1/2

2-1/2   8   2-1/2

1-1/2

*Perimeter Measurement is **8** cubits

Since the Ark of the Covenant bears the perimeter measurement of "8," this alone will tell us that we are on the right track to knowing how God looks at these measurements. The Ark is the main piece of furniture of the Tabernacle, and the number 8 is one of the key numbers, if not the key number of the Bible, for it represents our redemption in Christ.

We will discuss the number 8 in greater detail in chapter nine, but for now, it is important to understand that it is one of the main numbers of the Bible. It is as if God put His signature of Redemption on the Ark by giving it a measurement of eight.

You see, this system of adding up the measurements of the four sides brings forth a revelation of how the main piece of furniture of the Tabernacle bears one of the main numbers of the Bible, and this is certainly no coincidence. In searching for an understanding of the numbers and patterns of the Bible, it is essential to take note of signs coming together such as this. It confirms that we are on the right track to finding how God looks at the numbers and patterns that He has given in His Word.

THE MEASUREMENTS AND NUMBERS OF THE TABERNACLE FURNITURE

This same system of measurement, of adding the four sides to get the perimeter measurement, can then be applied to the other pieces of furniture of the Tabernacle except for the Laver and Menorah, in which no measurements were given.

* Altar of Burnt Offering (Exodus 27:1): 5 + 5 + 5 + 5 = 20
* Table or Showbread (Exodus 25:23): 2 + 1 + 2 + 1 = 6
* Altar of Incense (Exodus 30:1-2): 1 + 1 + 1 + 1 = 4

EVEN THOUGH NO MEASUREMENTS ARE GIVEN FOR THE Laver or the Menorah, the Menorah is unique in that there are still definite numbers associated with it, for this candlestick has seven lamps. So, the natural numerical value of the Menorah can be counted by assigning numerals 1 through 7 to each of the lamps and adding up each consecutive number of the seven lamps.

Here again, you can use the mathematical formula, *n (the first integer + the last integer)/2 = the sum,* or you can just add each numeral together to reach the sum, "1+2+3+4+5+6+7=28". When you add up the sum of the seven lamps, the numerical value of the Menorah would be "28".

Now put the measurements and numbers of all the furniture together, and the sum is amazing. It is important to remember that the Laver is unique among the pieces of furniture of the Tabernacle in that there are no measurements or numbers associated with it. Here are the measurements and numbers of the furniture going from the entrance of the Tabernacle and on through to the Holy of Holies:

The Tabernacle

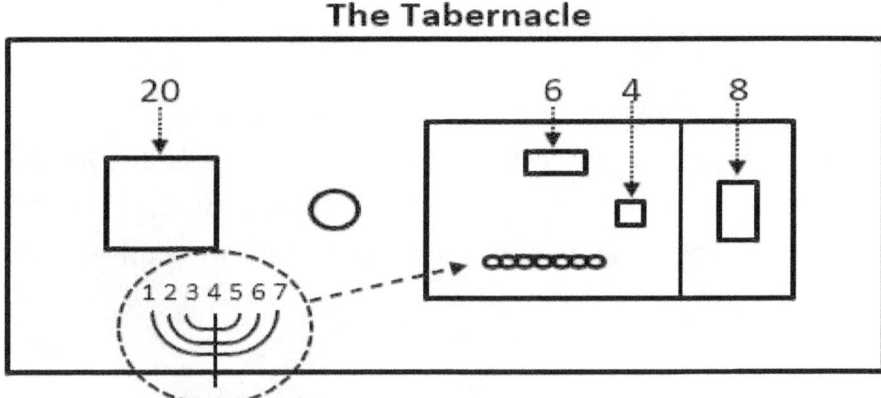

*Altar of Burnt Offering (Exodus 27:1): 5 + 5 + 5 + 5 = **20**
*Laver- No measurements or numbers were given.
*Table of Showbread (Exodus 25:23): 2 + 1 + 2 + 1 = **6**
*Menorah (Exodus 25:31-32): 1 + 2 + 3 + 4 + 5 + 6 + 7= **28**
*Altar of Incense (Exodus 30:1-2): 1 + 1 + 1 + 1 = **4**
*Ark (Exodus 25:8-22): 2 ½ + 1 ½ + 2 ½ + 1 ½ = **8**
Total Sum of the furniture: 20 + 6 + 28 + 4 + 8 = "66"

THE MEASUREMENTS AND NUMBERS OF THE FURNITURE reveal that the number "66" was even hidden in the pattern of the Tabernacle. Think about this for a moment. This is an extremely important number to God because it tells the testimony of His Son and how He won the victory over sin and death.

So, by placing this number 66 in the numbers of the tabernacle furniture, He not only gave testimony of Jesus but also, long before the Bible was entirely written or put together, God gave testimony of His foreknowledge and power to place the exact number of books in the Bible that He alone had chosen to be there.

THE NUMBER OF ABOMINATION "666"

When you understand just how significant the number 66 is to God and what this number means to Him, it then brings forth a revelation of why the number "666" is the number of the antichrist. The book of Revelation talks about the number 666 and describes it this way,

> "Here is wisdom. Let him who has understanding calculate the number of the beast, for it is the number of a man: His number is 666."
> (Revelation 13:18 NKJV)

The Bible says that the number of the beast (666) is the number of a "man." Since the number 66 declares the gospel of Jesus Christ, it is easy to see why the number of the antichrist is 666.

You see, the number 66 declares the first man (6) that failed and the second Man (6), the last Adam, Jesus Christ, who prevailed. So, 66 is a complete number declaring that Jesus has come in the flesh, finished the work, and won the victory over sin and death.

So, when you add another number 6, to the number that

already declares the victory of Jesus (the second Man), it is then a number of abomination. Since 6 is the number of man, then a third number 6, added to the number 66, is the sign of the antichrist who will be declaring that he is the savior of the world instead of Jesus.

Since the victory was complete in Jesus Christ, whom the Bible calls the second Man, then there is no place for another man (or a third man) to come and save us, and so there is no place for another 6 to be added to the number 66.

You see, when the antichrist comes onto the scene, he will deny Jesus Christ and proclaim himself to be the savior of the world. He is a man (6) who will proclaim himself as the Messiah and Christ. He will try to make everyone receive his mark, and the Bible tells us that all who receive the mark of the beast will spend eternity in the lake of fire.

In essence, to receive the number of his name, "666," is to deny that Jesus has come in the flesh to save us. To receive the number 666 would be like receiving the antichrist as your savior. Remember that in the book of 1st John, the Bible declares,

> "...and every spirit that does not confess that Jesus
> Christ has come in the flesh is not of God.
> And this is the spirit of the Antichrist, which
> you have heard was coming, and is now
> already in the world." (1st John 4:3 NKJV)

We are getting close to the end of time when Jesus will return. We know the Bible has foretold us that the antichrist will come on the scene in these end times. Many will be tempted to take the mark of the beast which bears the number 666, and those who take it will have their part in the lake of fire for eternity. The Bible has forewarned us not to take this mark, for it is only through Jesus that we are saved. Just as Jesus said,

"But he who endures to the end shall be saved."
(Matthew 24:13 NKJV)

CHAPTER 7

THE 3 MEASURES OF GOD'S PLAN OF REDEMPTION

GOD FASHIONED HIS WORD IN SUCH A WAY THAT ONE pattern builds upon another. We have been looking at the message of the first Adam and the last Adam, and how God used the Pattern of Seconds and the number 66 to signify this message. Taking it a step further, this message opened the door to another key pattern in God's Word, for it was the actions of the first Adam and the last Adam that revealed the "3 Measures of God's Plan of Redemption."

As we continue our journey up the stairsteps, there is a definite structure or pattern of three measures that is found in God's Word, and these three measures are the setting for His entire plan of our redemption in Christ. The first Measure (or time frame) is the "Perfect Creation," which is when God created everything perfect at the beginning. Yet this first Measure would only last until man sinned. Once Adam sinned, the Perfect Creation fell into the curse, darkness, sin, and death.

The world in its fallen state is the 2nd Measure, which I will call the "Fall of Man." This 2nd Measure is the fallen world we still see all around us. Man was separated from God's Rest because of sin, so a gap (or breach) of sin came between God and man.

Then God placed a Staircase right in the midst of this fallen world, and this Staircase is the only pathway to the 3rd Measure, which is "Redemption." This 3rd Measure is the wonderful salvation and deliverance from sin and death that we are invited into through the last Adam, Jesus Christ.

The transition from one measure to the next was a direct result of the first Adam and the last Adam, for it was the first Adam who sinned and brought us out of the Perfect Creation (the 1st Measure) and into the Fall of Man (the 2nd Measure). It was the last Adam, Jesus Christ, the Staircase, who paid the price for our sins and brought us out of the Fall of Man (the 2nd Measure) and into Redemption (the 3rd Measure).

Because of Adam's sin, every person starts off lost in this fallen world, which is the 2nd Measure, and it is only the Staircase that brings us into the 3rd Measure, Redemption. Therefore, God's entire plan of Redemption is based upon a pattern of 3 Measures: the Perfect Creation, the Fall of Man, and Redemption.

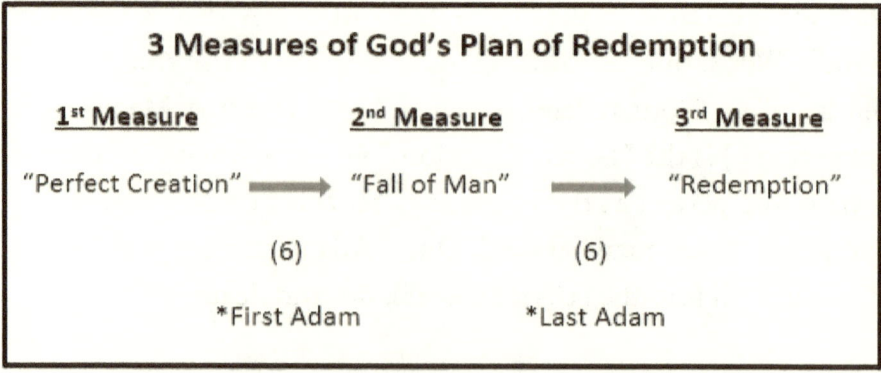

3 Measures of God's Plan of Redemption

1st Measure	2nd Measure	3rd Measure
"Perfect Creation" ⟶	"Fall of Man" ⟶	"Redemption"
(6)	(6)	
*First Adam	*Last Adam	

THE 3 MEASURES CONSIST OF A "NUMERICAL MAP"

The 3 Measures of God's Plan of Redemption also consist of a numerical pattern of His entire plan. It's as if God attached numbers to each of these 3 Measures. The foundation for this numerical "map" is found in the 1st Measure, the Perfect Creation.

In the first two chapters of the Bible, God gives us a numerical pattern, or, you could say, a numerical "map" of the world that He created. He framed the world in a time frame of 7 days. The Bible gives specific details of the six days of creation and how He rested from his perfect works on the 7th day.

When you write the numerals "1 through 7," it is a numerical map of the Perfect Creation that the Lord had made. In the following illustration, numbers "1 through 7" represent the 7 days of the Perfect Creation.

---

3 Measures of God's Plan of Redemption

1st Measure	2nd Measure	3rd Measure
"Perfect Creation"		
1 2 3 4 5 6 7		

THE NUMBER "1" REPRESENTS "GOD'S LIGHT"

It is important to identify the specific numbers that God chose to use in the Bible because He tells the gospel message even in using those numbers. We have seen how the number 7 represents God's

Rest because of what God did on the 7th day. So, the meaning of the number is based on what God did on that specific day of creation.

Following that same pattern, we must ask ourselves, "What did God do on the 1st day?" On the 1st day, He said, *Let there be light*. So, the primary focus of the 1st day is that God put His light into the creation. Just as the number 7 represents God's Rest because of what He did on the 7th day, so also, the number 1 represents "God's Light" because of what He did on the 1st day.

BOOKENDS OF THE CREATION

The numbers 1 and 7 are like the bookends of God's Perfect Creation. On the 1st day, He said, "Let there be light," and there was light. Then He made the whole creation in subjection to that light, and so it was perfect. Since everything was subject to His Light, it was, therefore, in His Rest. So, the numbers 1 and 7 are like the bookends of God's Perfect Creation because they are found at the beginning and the end, and they declare that everything was very good and blessed being in His Light "1" and in His Rest "7."

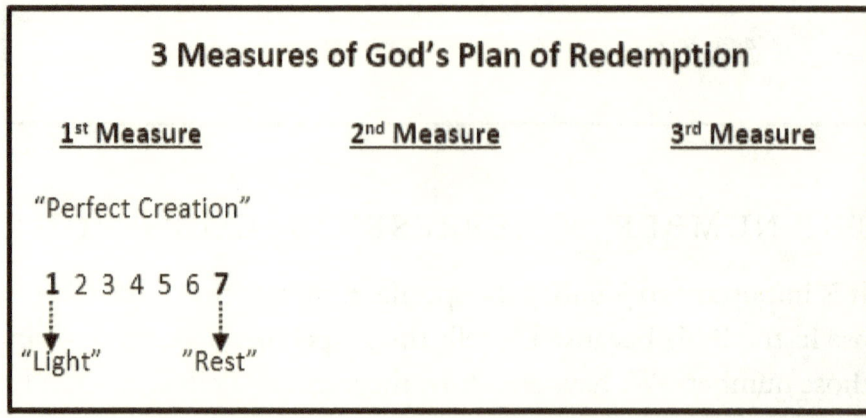

Numbers 1 through 7 show the Perfect Creation of 7 days (the 1st Measure) in a numerical form or map. Then, for the remaining two measures, there will also be a new set of numbers 1 through 7 written to show each new time frame of the world. This will make a total of 3 groups of 7: one group of 7 for each of the 3 Measures of God's Plan of Redemption.

Remember that each group of 7 depicts a different stage, or time frame, of the world that is based on the sin of the first Adam, who brought us out of the Perfect Creation and into the Fall of Man, and the love of the last Adam, Jesus Christ, who brought us out of the Fall of Man and gave us Redemption.

THE 2ND MEASURE: FALL OF MAN

Once man sinned, God's Light (1) went out of man's heart, and the curse, darkness, sin, and death passed upon the creation that was made in 6 days, and so the whole creation was separated from God's Rest (7). We will now look at an illustration of the 2nd Measure of the 7 days of creation: the present world in its fallen state.

In this second group of 7 days, I am inserting the symbol of the "/gap/" in between the 6th and 7th day to illustrate the gap (or breach) that came in between the 6 days of creation and God's Rest (7). This "/gap/" shows the separation between God and His creation once sin had entered in, and God's Light from the first day had gone out of the creation. It defines the price that would have to be met for man to reach Him again.

---

3 Measures of God's Plan of Redemption

1st Measure	2nd Measure	3rd Measure
"Perfect Creation" ⟹	"Fall of Man"	
1 2 3 4 5 6 **7**	1 2 3 4 5 6 /gap/ **7**	
*First (6) Adam		

THE 3RD MEASURE: REDEMPTION

Man, along with the whole creation, was separated from God's Rest (7). There was now a "/gap/," or breach, between God and His creation because of sin. Yet God's Plan of Redemption was made known from the beginning. From the time that man sinned, even while Adam was still in the garden of Eden, God gave a promise of the Seed that was to come and bruise the serpent's head and deliver us from the curse, darkness, sin, and death.

To illustrate the 3rd Measure, Redemption, I will write a 3rd group of numerals 1 through 7, depicting the 7 days of creation that are reconciled through the last Adam, Jesus Christ.

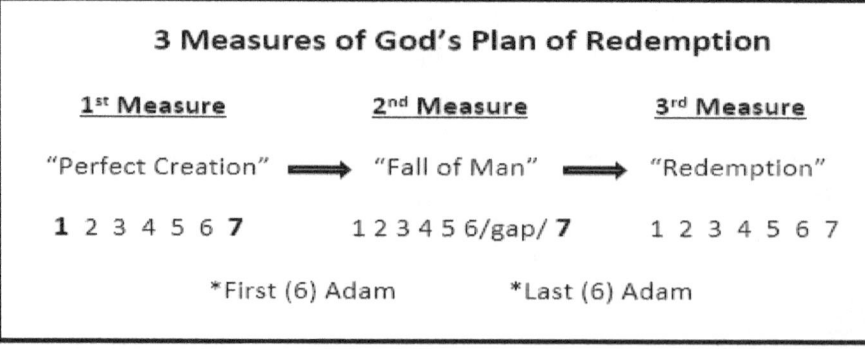

3 Measures of God's Plan of Redemption

1st Measure	2nd Measure	3rd Measure
"Perfect Creation" ⟹	"Fall of Man" ⟹	"Redemption"
1 2 3 4 5 6 **7**	1 2 3 4 5 6/gap/ **7**	1 2 3 4 5 6 7
*First (6) Adam	*Last (6) Adam	

ONE ADDITIONAL NUMBER IN THE 3RD MEASURE

This 3rd group of 7 days, which declares Redemption, has an additional number that the previous two groups of 7 did not contain. For God gave us the number that is beyond His 7th day Rest to declare the ultimate fulfillment of His plan of Redemption in Christ.

You see, the 3rd group of 7 days declares that when Jesus came, He brought the perfect works of God back to the creation, thereby reconciling the creation. Yet when Jesus came to save us, He did not only reconcile the original 7 days of the creation, but His Redemption brings us beyond those 7 days, and into the new heaven and earth to come. As it is written in the Book of Revelation,

> "Now I saw a new heaven and a new earth, for the
> first heaven and the first earth had passed
>
> away...." (Revelation 21:1, NKJV)

The original creation had to do with 7 days, but the new heaven and earth to come are represented by the number that is beyond the 7 days of the original creation. For 7 days alone are not adequate to represent the 3rd Measure which is our Redemption in Christ.

In other words, a group of only 7 days in the 3rd Measure could not cover the scope of the magnificent deliverance that Jesus accomplished when He came in the flesh. So, the Lord gave us a number "beyond" 7, which is the number of Redemption, and that number is 8. Therefore, this 3rd Measure consists of numbers 1 through 8, declaring the fullness of our Redemption through the Staircase, Jesus Christ.

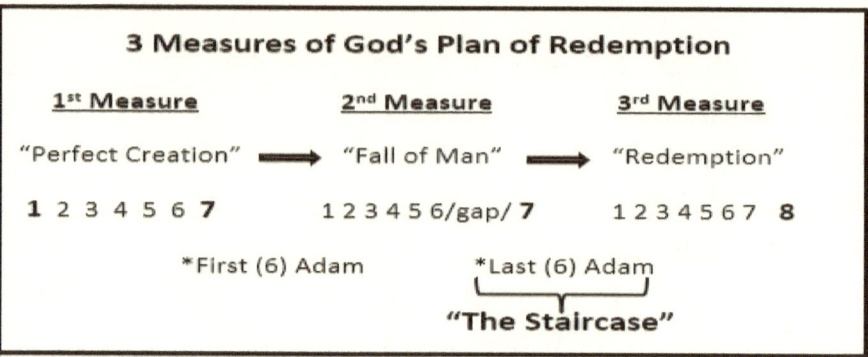

These 3 Measures (or time frames) are the setting of God's entire plan of Redemption in Christ. It is important to note that this numerical map, which is made up of 3 groups of 7 days, with the 3rd group extending through the 8th day (a total of 22 days), can be found in several places in the Bible. It's located in the 22 cups of the Menorah (Exodus 25:31-40), the account of Noah's Ark, and can even be found twice in the Feasts of the Lord, being most easily recognized in the Feasts of the 7th month, which take place in a period of "22 days".

Every time this pattern of 3 Measures is found, God was declaring that there was a Perfect Creation which man lost, and how Jesus (the Staircase) crossed the "/gap/" that no one else could cross so that we could be redeemed to the Father.

Now let's look at how this 3rd Measure, Redemption, has both a "Now" and "Later" fulfillment. You see, God didn't make us wait until later to experience His wonderful Plan of Redemption. No, as believers, we get to experience the 3rd

Measure, "Redemption," right now while we are still in this fallen world.

CHAPTER 8

NOW AND LATER FULFILLMENT

WITHIN GOD'S GREAT PLAN OF REDEMPTION, HE provided a "Now" and "Later" fulfillment so that we would not have to wait until later to experience His Redemption. No, He made Redemption available to us right "Now" by giving us the opportunity to be born again through the Holy Spirit, thereby letting us walk in the Kingdom of God even while we are still in this fallen world.

Jesus, the Staircase, showed up right in the midst of this fallen world and ushered in His all-powerful Kingdom, making it available to all who believe. Yet this was not a visible Kingdom that could be seen, but an unseen, invisible Kingdom of spirit and truth.

In the 3 Measures of God's Plan of Redemption, the 3rd Measure, "Redemption," is synonymous with the Kingdom of God. This 3rd Measure, Redemption, has both a Now and Later fulfillment, which declares that the Kingdom of God is available right "Now" in spirit and truth. Then it will be fully manifested "Later" in the visible realm for all to see when Jesus returns.

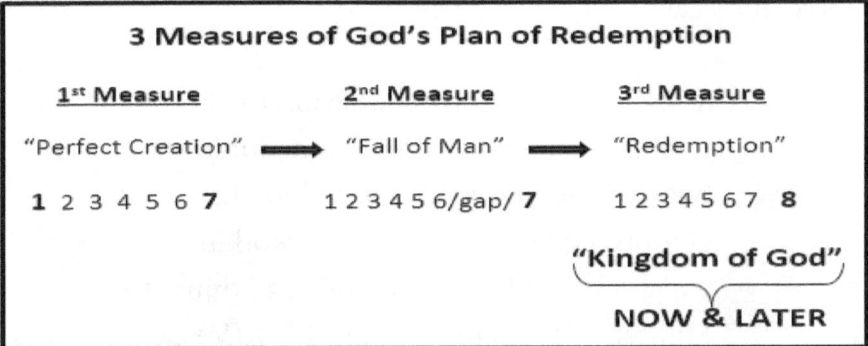

THE "NOW" FULFILLMENT

Even though we still see the fallen world all around us, Redemption is available to us right "Now" in the Spirit because Jesus has given us the opportunity to be born again through the Holy Spirit, which makes us free to walk in the Kingdom of God and worship Him in spirit and truth. As Jesus described,

> "But the hour is coming, and now is, when the
> true worshipers will worship the Father in
> spirit and truth; for the Father is seeking such
> to worship Him. God is Spirit, and those who
> worship Him must worship in spirit and
> truth." (John 4:23-24 NKJV)

. . .

THE "LATER" FULFILLMENT

Then the fullness of our Redemption will come "Later" in the flesh when we receive a glorified body, at which time the Kingdom of God will be fully manifested on this earth in the visible, physical realm. As Paul described,

> "...we also eagerly wait for the Savior, the Lord
> Jesus Christ, who will transform our lowly
> body that it may be conformed to His
> glorious body, according to the working by
> which He is able even to subdue all things to
> Himself." (Philippians 3:20-21 NKJV) .

Paul also describes this Now and Later fulfillment of Redemption in Romans 8:15 and 23 by using the word "adoption." He explains that we have received the adoption, and then goes on to say that we are still waiting for the adoption. How can it be that we have received the adoption and can still be waiting for it too?

He explains that there is a fulfillment that occurs "Now" in the Spirit, and there is a fullness that occurs "Later" in the flesh. In verse 15, he says that we have received the *Spirit of adoption.* Then, in verse 23, he says that we are still waiting for the adoption, and then goes on to explain the adoption that we are still *waiting for* as being *the redemption of our body.* So, the "Now" fulfillment of Redemption is in the Spirit, and the "Later" fulfillment of Redemption is in the body, the flesh.

It is just the same with the Kingdom of God. We are invited to walk in the Kingdom of God right "Now" in the Spirit, and then His Kingdom will be fully manifested in this visible physical realm "Later." Paul spoke of this same point in Colossians 1:26-27 as the mystery hidden through the ages, and he defines this mystery as "Christ in you the hope of glory." This one statement reveals both the Now and Later fulfillment.

He was revealing that we can "Now" have Christ in us when we are born again, enabling us to walk in the Kingdom of God right now in this visible fallen world as we continue in the hope of that future glory that comes "Later." This future *glory* is not only the time in which we will receive a glorified body, but it is also the time that the Kingdom of God will be fully manifested on this earth.

So, the "Now" fulfillment of Redemption takes place in the midst of this fallen world as believers in Christ are presently able to walk in the Kingdom of God, while the "Later" fulfillment of Redemption begins when we receive our glorified body.

THE PHARISEES DID NOT UNDERSTAND THE "NOW" AND "LATER" FULFILLMENT

In the time of Jesus, the Pharisees were waiting for the Messiah, but they did not understand that there would be a 1st and 2nd Coming of the Messiah. They did not understand that there was a Now and Later fulfillment of His Plan of Redemption. They were looking for the "Later" fulfillment only.

They were waiting on the Messiah, but they thought the Messiah would make the Kingdom of God "immediately" appear in the physical realm. Yet, Jesus knew what they were thinking, and He explained to them that the Kingdom of God would first be given without observation in the physical realm. Jesus said,

...The Kingdom of God does not come with observation; nor will they say, 'See here!' or 'See there!' For indeed, the Kingdom of God is within you. (Luke 17:20-21 NKJV)

Jesus was explaining that at His first coming, He was here to make His Kingdom available in spirit and truth. Then His Kingdom will be fully manifested Later in the physical realm for all to see when He returns at His second coming.

THE SAME MESSIAH

The Jewish people are still waiting for their Messiah to come and do "the same thing" that we, as Christians, are waiting on Jesus to come and do at His 2nd coming, which is to rule and reign in the visible physical realm on this earth. That is because both Jews and Christians are waiting on **the same** Messiah, Jesus Christ.

The Book of Isaiah, Chapter 53, paints a clear picture of the 1st coming of the Messiah, and how the Messiah would suffer for our sins. Jesus fulfilled the suffering in His 1st coming, when He went to the cross, at which time He made the Kingdom of God available in the Spirit for all who will believe. At His 2nd coming, His glory will fully manifest for all to see.

So, this treasure of the Kingdom of God is available "Now" in spirit and truth for those who will believe, and "Later," His Kingdom will be fully manifested on this earth at His return. We must all receive Jesus as our Savior while it is in the "Now," while it is called "Today" (Hebrews 3:15) so that we will be able to spend eternity with Him in the "Later" fulfillment.

"...Behold, now is the accepted time; behold, now is the day of salvation." (2nd Corinthians 6:2 NKJV)

Also, as the Book of Isaiah says, "Seek the Lord while He may be found, call upon Him while He is near" (Isaiah 55:6 NKJV).

THE INVISIBLE KINGDOM

What is this wonderful Kingdom that we have been invited into? It is the unseen, invisible, all-powerful spirit realm of God over which Jesus reigns as King, and it is called the Kingdom of God. This Kingdom declares the absolute authority of Jesus, the Word of God, who created everything. Hebrews 11:3 lets us in on this revelation of how it was the invisible that made the visible.

> "By faith we understand that the worlds were
>   framed by the word of God, so that the things
>   which are seen were not made of things
>   which are visible." (NKJV)

Jesus, the Staircase, came to overcome the devil and his kingdom of darkness that was ruling over us. He came to bring the unseen, invisible, all-powerful Kingdom of God into this visible fallen world, just as the Bible says in Mark 1:14-15,

> ".... Jesus came to Galilee, preaching the gospel of
>   the Kingdom of God, and saying, 'The time is
>   fulfilled, and the Kingdom of God is at hand.
>   Repent, and believe in the gospel.'" (NKJV)

On one occasion, when Jesus had cast a demon out, He explained to the people that "...the Kingdom of God has come upon you" (Luke 11:20 NKJV). When He sent the disciples to heal the sick, He told them to let the people know that the Kingdom of God had come near them.

In Luke 11:21-23, Jesus described His victory over the kingdom of darkness in this way,

> "When a strong man, fully armed, guards his own
> palace, his goods are in peace. But when a
> stronger than he comes upon him and
> overcomes him, he takes from him all of his
> armor in which he trusted, and divides his
> spoils. He who is not with Me is against Me,
> and he who does not gather with Me
> scatters." (NKJV)

Jesus brought His Kingdom to overcome this physical world through the power of the Holy Spirit. He came to deliver us from all the oppression of the devil (Acts 10:38), and to turn us from darkness to light, and from the power of Satan to God (Acts 26:18). He not only came to overcome the darkness, but to also invite us into His glorious Kingdom. Jesus said,

> "Do not fear, little flock, for it is your Father's
> good pleasure to give you the kingdom."
> (Luke 12:32 NKJV)

You see, Jesus came right into Satan's territory, where the kingdom of darkness had a stronghold over us because of sin and death, and He stripped Him of all power. In Colossians 2:15, the Bible explains that Jesus came and "disarmed principalities and powers." What an amazing gift that we are now invited to live in the Kingdom of the King who has already *disarmed* the enemy.

Jesus showed up right in the midst of this fallen world and ushered in His all-powerful Kingdom, making it presently available to all who will believe. Right "Now" we can live in His Kingdom while the rest of the world has no access to Him unless they choose to believe.

MANIFESTED TO BELIEVERS NOW, BUT NOT TO THE WORLD

In John 14:21-27, one of the disciples asked Jesus a fundamental question. He asked, "...Lord, how is it that you will manifest yourself to us, and not the world?" *(NKJV)*.

I believe this disciple was getting a glimpse of understanding of how Jesus would make His Kingdom available to believers in this fallen world, while nonbelievers would have no access to it. He was asking Jesus how believers would partake of His Kingdom, while the rest of the world does not. Jesus answered him and told him that the way that He was going to manifest Himself to believers and not to the world was by giving us the Holy Spirit. In verse 23, Jesus said,

> "...If anyone loves Me, he will keep My word, and
> My Father will love him, and We will come to
> him and make Our home with him." (NKJV)

In saying this, Jesus was speaking of the Holy Spirit, whom

the Father would give to all who believe in Him. A few verses earlier, in verses 16 & 17, Jesus said (while speaking of the Holy Spirit),

> "...for He dwells with you and will be in you."
> (NKJV)

So, in the "Now" fulfillment of Redemption, which takes place in this fallen world, how does Jesus make His Kingdom available to us? How does Jesus give us the Kingdom, and at the same time, make it inaccessible to those in this world who don't believe? He manifests His Kingdom to believers by giving us the Holy Spirit in the midst of this fallen world, and only those who have been cleansed by the blood of Jesus can receive the Holy Spirit.

Therefore, in the 3 Measures of God's Plan of Redemption, it is the 3rd Measure (Redemption) that God uses to declare the amazing unseen, invisible, all-powerful Kingdom of God that is available right now for all who choose the Staircase, Jesus Christ.

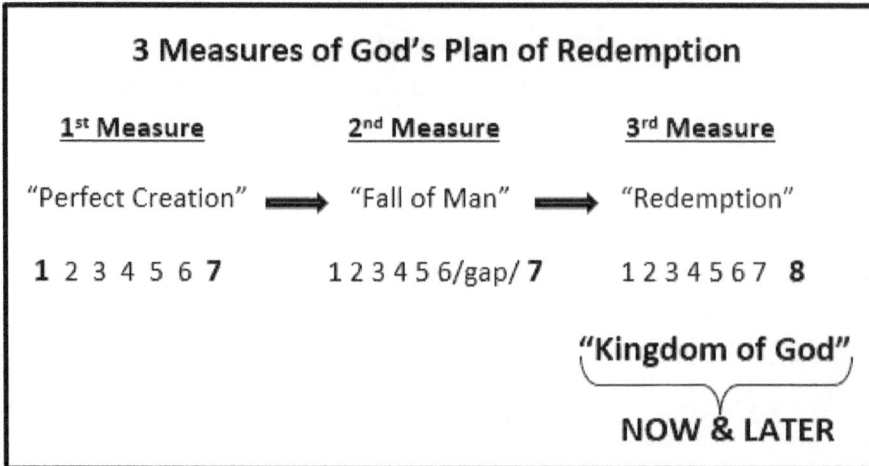

CHAPTER 9

"8" IS THE NUMBER OF REDEMPTION

As we saw in the 3 Measures of God's Plan of Redemption, the number 8 declares the fullness of God's Plan of Redemption through Jesus Christ. Since God's Plan of Redemption extends beyond the reconciliation of the 7 days of creation, God used the number that was beyond the 7th day, the number 8, to declare the ultimate fulfillment of His plan.

THE NUMBER 8 DECLARES NEW BEGINNINGS

God's mighty work of Redemption consists of a series of "new beginnings," all three represented by the number 8 in the Bible. One of the inherent characteristics of God's Redemption is that it always declares a "new beginning" in Christ. Just as the day after the 7th day of a week is the start of a new week, so also God used the 8th day to declare that His plan of Redemption would allow us to start over and have a new beginning in Christ.

There was a "new beginning" when Jesus rose from the grave

on the 3rd day through the power of the Holy Spirit and became the firstborn from the grave. This gave every person the opportunity to have a "new beginning" in Christ by being born again of the Spirit. Then, ultimately there will be a "new beginning" at the end when all of those who are born again through Jesus will enter the "new" heaven and earth which is to come. All three of these new beginnings were signified in the Bible by the number 8. Now let's take a closer look at each one.

"8" IS SYNONYMOUS WITH THE "3RD DAY" THAT JESUS ROSE

God used the 8th day to declare the resurrection of Jesus, for the 8th day is synonymous with the 3rd day in which He rose from the grave. To find this understanding, it is essential to remember that the 3rd day (counting from the cross) landed on the first day of the new week, which was a Sunday, and Sunday is the day after the Sabbath day (Luke 24:1,21).

Also, it is vital to understand how the "3rd day" is counted in the Bible. In the Bible, the 3rd day is always counted as the day after tomorrow. In other words, it is counted as "today" being the first day, "tomorrow" being the 2nd day, and the day after tomorrow is then counted as the 3rd day (Exodus 19:10-11, Luke 13:32).

Therefore, counting from His death on the cross, Jesus died on the day before the Sabbath day (day 1), then His body laid in the grave the entire Sabbath day (day 2), and then He rose from the grave the day after the Sabbath day, which was the 3rd day. Here is a chart of the days of the week that shows the biblical counting of the 3rd day. Remember that in biblical times Sunday was the first day of the week.

Days of the Week Chart

Sunday /	Mon. /	Tues. /	Wed. /	Thurs. /	Fri. /	Sat. /	Sunday
1	2	3	4	5	6	7	"1"

*Counting from the Cross——➤ 1st   2nd   **3rd Day**

This is where a hidden revelation of the number 8 can be found in God's Word. The revelation is that the number 8 is synonymous with the 3rd day that Jesus rose from the grave. Instead of starting the counting of the week over with the "1st day" of the new week, you simply extend the count of the 7 days (counting consecutively), and the 1st day of the new week becomes the "8th day".

Days of the Week Chart

Sunday /	Mon. /	Tues. /	Wed. /	Thurs. /	Fri. /	Sat. /	Sunday
1	2	3	4	5	6	7	"8"

*Counting from the Cross——➤ 1st   2nd   **3rd Day**

Therefore, God used the number 8 in the Old Testament as a hidden revelation that spoke of the 3rd day, on which Jesus would rise from the grave and become the firstborn from the dead.

THE PROMISE OF THE HOLY SPIRIT

God not only used the number 8 to declare the resurrection of Jesus, but He also used that same number (which is the day beyond 7) to declare that through Jesus, we would have a "new beginning" by receiving the Promise of the Holy Spirit. In the book of John, Jesus directly connected the gift of the Holy Spirit with the "8th day" of the Feast of Tabernacles.

The last day of the Feast of Tabernacles was referred to as "the great day," which was the "8th day of the Feast" (Leviticus 23:36). It was on this 8th day of the Feast that Jesus stood and spoke about giving the Holy Spirit to those who believe in Him,

> "On the last day, that great day of the feast, Jesus
> stood and cried out, saying, 'If anyone thirsts,
> let him come to Me and drink. He who
> believes in Me, as the Scripture has said, out
> of his heart will flow rivers of living water.'
> But this He spoke concerning the Spirit,
> whom those believing in Him would receive;
> for the Holy Spirit was not yet given, because
> Jesus was not yet glorified." (John 7:37-39
> NKJV)

So, it was on the "8th day" of the Feast that Jesus spoke of giving the Holy Spirit to those who believe in Him. Again, God used the number beyond 7 to declare a "new beginning." This time it was "our" new beginning in Jesus Christ when we receive the Promise of the Holy Spirit. This new birth through the Holy Spirit will ultimately lead to our entrance into the "new" heaven and earth to come, which is also represented by the number 8 since it is the number that is beyond the original creation of 7 days.

Therefore, the number 8 declares God's overall plan of Redemption. How that God would raise Jesus from the dead on the 3rd day through the power of the Holy Spirit, which would then allow us to receive the promise of the Holy Spirit, "Christ in us the hope of glory" (Colossians 1:27), which not only reconciles us to the Father, but goes beyond this creation of 7 days, and brings us into the new heaven and earth to come.

THE NUMBER 8 IN THE OLD TESTAMENT

Just like a picture is worth a thousand words, God used the number 8 to speak a thousand words. It was like a numerical signature that God used to show the hidden mystery of our Redemption through Jesus Christ from the beginning.

When you understand that God chose to designate His overall plan of Redemption with this specific number, it is easy to see why God used the number 8 in so many key places throughout the Old Testament. Every time it was to signify His Plan of Redemption that would be made available through the Staircase, Jesus Christ.

There were 8 people saved on Noah's Ark. The Covenant of Circumcision that God made with Abraham took place on the 8th day. God's glory appeared to Moses and the Children of Israel on the 8th day (Leviticus 9:1,23). It was on the 8th day that an offering was made for an atonement (Numbers 6:9-11). It was also on the 8th day and thereafter, that an animal would be accepted as an offering (Exodus 22:30/ Leviticus 22:27). In

Ezekiel's vision of the Temple, it was on the 8th day and thereafter that a person would be accepted by the Lord (Ezekiel 43:27).

In the Law, a leper was to bring an offering on the 8th day for his cleansing (Leviticus 14:23). Jesus even made a reference back to that specific offering after He healed a man of leprosy. He told him to go offer this offering to the priests as a "testimony to them" (Luke 5:12-14). For He was declaring that He is the fulfillment of what this offering described, and this offering had to do with the 8th day. Here again, God chose the "8th" day to be used as a testimony of Jesus.

It was in the 8th month that the Temple of Solomon was finished, and it was this Temple that Jesus revealed as a foreshadowing of Himself (John 2:19-22). Also, it was on the 8th day of the Feast that Solomon sent the people away joyful and glad of heart for all the good that the Lord had done. So, God used the 8th day to paint a picture of how we can now go forth in this world joyful and glad of heart for all the good that Jesus has done, for the 8th day represents our Redemption in Christ.

THE ARK AND THE NUMBER 8

As we saw in chapter six, even the Ark of the Covenant bears the number 8 in measurement. Since God connected the Ark with the number 8, it is important to realize that every time the Ark was mentioned, God was also speaking of the number 8 as well, thereby declaring His overall Plan of Redemption in Christ.

It was this Ark that was placed behind the veil in the Most Holy Place of the Tabernacle. The Bible says that Jesus entered the Most Holy Place having obtained "eternal redemption for us" (Hebrews 9:12), and so this Ark, which bears the number 8 in measurement, was used to signify our Redemption in Christ. In essence, God was saying that Redemption (8) was hidden behind the veil and was not available to us until Jesus came and took the veil away.

This same Ark of the Covenant also stood in the Jordan River as Israel passed over into the Promised Land. By placing the Ark (which bears the number 8 in measurement) in the Jordan, He was declaring that Jesus would rise from the grave and give us the Holy Spirit so that we could enter into the true Promised Land Rest of God. He was declaring our Redemption in Christ.

The Ark also circled Jericho before the walls fell by the power of God. Since the Ark bears the number 8 in measurement, God was declaring that it was through everything the number 8 represents that the walls fell. In other words, it is only through Jesus and the gift of the Holy Spirit that we can take the land. Again, God used the number 8 to declare the victory and Redemption in Jesus.

Also, when the Children of Israel moved from one location to another in the wilderness, it was when the Ark set out that Moses would say, "...Rise up, O Lord! Let Your enemies be scattered...." (Numbers 10:35 NKJV). Even this was a hidden mystery that spoke of the resurrection of Jesus, how Jesus would one day rise from the grave, causing His enemies to be scattered.

So, when Moses said those words in connection with the Ark, God was using him to declare that it would be through Jesus and the Holy Spirit that all of God's enemies would be scattered. Remember that Jesus said,

"He who is not with Me is against Me, and he who does not gather with Me scatters." (Luke 11:23 NKJV)

Following this same line of thought of how the Ark of the Covenant bears the number 8 in measurement, let's look again at the illustration or "map" of the 3 Measures of God's Plan of Redemption. Remember that it was the 3rd group of 7 that extends through the number 8, because the 3rd Measure represents "Redemption."

Since the Ark is rectangular (from an overhead view), I have inserted a rectangle around the number 8 in the map of the "3 Measures of God's Plan of Redemption" from now on. This rectangle around the number 8 signifies how the Ark of the Covenant lines up directly with the number 8 in the "3 Measures of God's Plan of Redemption" because both the Ark and the number 8 carry the same message of our Redemption in Christ.

---

3 Measures of God's Plan of Redemption

1st Measure	2nd Measure	3rd Measure
"Perfect Creation" ➡	"Fall of Man" ➡	"Redemption"
1 2 3 4 5 6 7	1 2 3 4 5 6/gap/ 7	1 2 3 4 5 6 7 8
		ARK

Throughout the entire Old Testament, God used the number 8 to declare His overall plan of Redemption, and to reveal the invisible, all-powerful Kingdom of God that we have now been invited into through the Staircase, Jesus Christ.

CHAPTER 10

THE MENORAH

As we continue walking up the steps of the Staircase, all of God's numbers, patterns, and symbols fit precisely together and build upon one another. We have just seen how the Ark of the Covenant lines up directly with the 3rd Measure, Redemption. There is also another piece of furniture in the Tabernacle of Moses that lines up directly with the 3rd Measure: the Menorah.

God always causes one pattern to build upon another. As we will see in a later chapter, it is not only the furniture, but also the entire Tabernacle that serves as a "map" of our Redemption and lays upon the same structure of the 3 Measures of God's Plan of Redemption. For now, we will only focus on the Menorah and the Ark.

Together, these two pieces of furniture in the Tabernacle give us a foundation of understanding and help us lay hold of the meaning of the numbers and patterns of the Bible. They not only declare the 3rd Measure, Redemption, but these two pieces of furniture were also used to reveal the Kingdom of God that has been made available to us right now amid this fallen world through the Staircase, Jesus Christ.

The Menorah was one of the primary symbols of the Old Testament, and it speaks of all that Jesus would accomplish. It was the golden candlestick with 7 lamps that stood in the Tabernacle. It consisted of 1 center candlestick with 6 branches (Exodus 25:31-32). Just as the Ark lines up with the 8th day of the 3rd Measure, the Menorah lines up with the 7 days of the 3rd Measure.

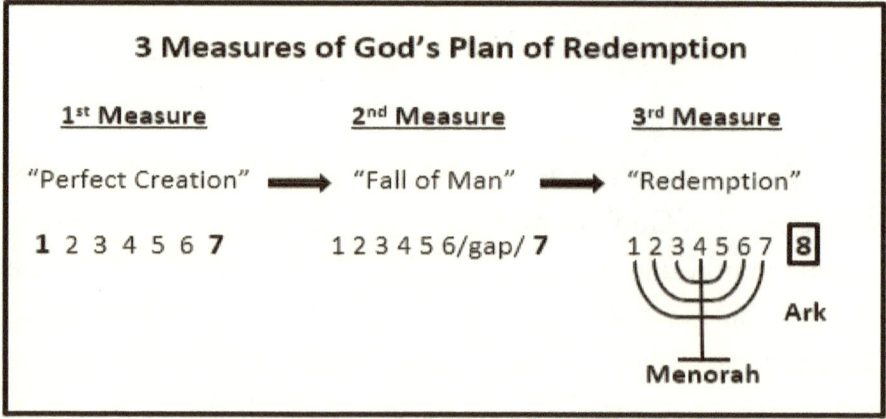

THE 7 LAMPS OF THE MENORAH AND THE 7 DAYS OF CREATION

The first place in the Bible where God used the numerical count of 7 was in the 7 days of the Perfect Creation. Since all of God's numbers and patterns go together, it stands to reason that these 7 lamps of the Menorah would have something to do with the 7 days of the Perfect Creation. To understand the meaning of the Menorah and its connection to the 7 days of creation, we must first look at the room of the Tabernacle in which it was placed, as compared to the room of the Tabernacle in which the Ark was placed.

THE HOLY PLACE AND THE MOST HOLY PLACE

In the Tabernacle, the Tent of Meeting was divided into two parts. The first room was called the Holy Place, and the second room, behind the veil, was named the Most Holy Place or the Holy of Holies. So, these two rooms were separated by the veil, as stated in Exodus 26:33,

> "...The veil shall be a divider for you between the
> holy place and the Most Holy." (NKJV)

So, the veil was used to divide the two rooms, and this division declared the gospel of Jesus, how the way into the Presence of God was not available until Jesus came.

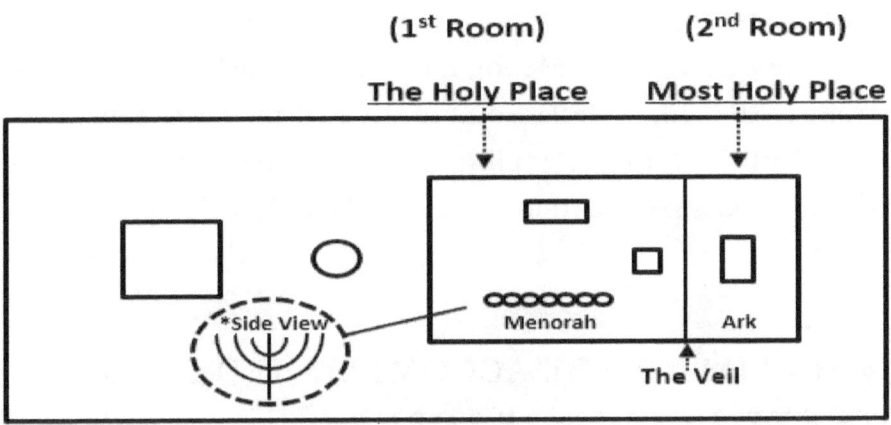

The Bible describes this in Hebrews 9:7-8, and says that by

separating the Holy Place from the Most Holy Place with the veil, that the Holy Spirit was telling us,

> "...that the way into the Holiest of All was not yet made manifest while the first tabernacle was still standing." (NKJV)

THE PLACEMENT OF THE MENORAH IN COMPARISON TO THE ARK

The Menorah was placed in the room which was "in front" of the veil, and the Ark was placed in the room "behind" the veil. The placement of these two pieces of furniture in relation to the veil is crucial in understanding the meaning of the Menorah.

The Ark, which bears the number 8 in measurement, was placed behind the veil to declare that our Redemption through Jesus was not yet available until Jesus came in the flesh and tore the veil. In other words, we could not receive the promise of the Holy Spirit until Jesus.

The 7 lamps of the Menorah stood in the room, which was in front of the veil, to declare and testify that there was something that Jesus had to accomplish before the veil could be torn, thereby making the entrance into the Most Holy Place available to all.

WHAT HAD TO BE ACCOMPLISHED BEFORE THE VEIL COULD BE TORN?

What did Jesus have to accomplish before the veil could be torn, making the Most Holy Place accessible to all who believe? He had to accomplish "the works" that His Father had sent Him to "finish." In John 5:36, Jesus said,

> "But I have a greater witness than John's; for the
> works which the Father has given Me to finish
> —the very works that I do—bear witness of
> Me, that the Father has sent Me." (NKJV)

He had to come in the flesh as the spotless lamb of God, live a perfect life full of the power of the Holy Spirit, and then pay the price for all our sins. In doing this, He brought God's perfect works of the original 7 days (which had been lost by man) back to the creation.

Just as there were 7 days of the Perfect Creation, so God gave Moses the instructions to make 7 lamps of the Menorah. Those 7 lamps declared the perfect works of creation that were lost, that Jesus would come and bring back with His own blood.

The 7 lamps of the Menorah stood in the room in front of the veil and gave testimony of the "Finished Works of Christ" that Jesus would accomplish so that the veil could be torn (Mark 15:38), and we could have access to the Most Holy Place. What had to be accomplished before the veil could be torn? It was the Finished Works of Christ that had to be accomplished, and so the Menorah declares the Finished Works of Christ.

IT IS FINISHED

When Jesus was on the cross, He said, "It is finished!" (John 19:30). What was finished? The works that His Father had given Him to accomplish. Then the veil of the Temple (which is the same symbol as the veil of the Tabernacle) was torn in two, declaring that the way into the Most Holy Place was now available through Jesus. God was declaring that through Jesus's death on the cross, there is no longer a veil between God and His creation, but that Redemption is now available to all who believe in Jesus.

Therefore, the Menorah (which stood in the room in front of the veil) declared the Finished Works of Christ that Jesus would accomplish to take away the veil. Removing this veil gave us access to the room where the Ark was kept, and the Ark represented our Redemption in Christ. So, the Ark specifically declares our "Redemption" in Christ, while the Menorah declares the "Finished Works of Christ," which had to be accomplished before we could receive His plan of Redemption.

"The Finished Works of Christ"

THE FINISHED WORKS OF CHRIST

To better understand the Finished Works of Christ, we must look back at what was lost. In Genesis 1:31, after God had made the

Perfect Creation, He saw that it was very *good.* So, when man sinned and ate from the tree, man lost the good and perfect works of God. Then, God sent His Son to bring His *goodness* back to the creation. Just as Acts 10:38 says,

> "How God anointed Jesus of Nazareth with the
> Holy Spirit and with power, who went about
> doing good and healing all who were
> oppressed by the devil for God was with
> Him." (NKJV)

So, it was Jesus Christ, the Staircase, that came to earth as a man and went about *doing good.* He lived a perfect life, and He was the only man who could receive the promise of the Holy Spirit. He flawlessly operated in the power of the Holy Spirit, and personally brought God's perfection and goodness back to the creation again. Then He paid the price for our sins with His own blood so that we, too, could receive the promise of the Holy Spirit.

Psalm 62:11 says,

> "God has spoken once, Twice I have heard this:
> That power belongs to God." (NKJV)

When Jesus brought God's perfect works back to the creation again, this was the "twice" that is spoken of in Psalm 62:11. Jesus brought the perfect works of God back to the creation the "second time," but this time, it was through His own blood.

This was God's Plan of Redemption through Jesus from the foundation of the world. When Jesus brought the good and perfect works of God back to His creation by living a perfect life and by shedding His blood, he accomplished the works that His Father had sent Him to finish (John 4:34), and His obedience to His Father's plan is called the "Finished Works of Christ."

HEALING AND THE FINISHED WORKS OF CHRIST

Every healing is a demonstration of the Finished Works of Christ. In John 9:3-4, the disciples asked Jesus why this man was born blind. Jesus explained to them that it was not for the reason they had thought it was. He said that it was not the blind man's sin or that of his parents, but that the *works of God* would be revealed in him. So, He began speaking to them about the Finished Works of Christ.

Jesus knew that all tribulation came into this world due to the first man's sin, and He was telling them that instead of trying to figure out the "why," they should focus on the answer. He was saying that He Himself is the answer, and that He was there to work this for good, and to bring God's perfect works "back" to the creation through His own blood.

Think about this. God originally made Adam from dust. You could break that down further and say that God made Adam's eyes from the dust. In John 9, the Bible says that Jesus made clay (He spit in the dust) and put the clay on the blind man's eyes. Jesus was showing that He was there to re-make this man's eyes the way they were intended to be in the garden of Eden. He was declaring that He was present to bring God's perfect works back to the creation.

The man followed Jesus's instructions and went to wash his eyes in the pool of Siloam (which means sent), and he was healed of blindness because Jesus was sent to bring the perfect works of God back to the creation.

Every time a person is healed, the Finished Works of Christ have been manifested. For every healing is simply God bringing His perfect works back to this fallen world through the blood of Jesus. Every time that Jesus forgave sins, cast out demons, or healed the sick, it was a manifestation of the works that His Father had given Him to accomplish, which would ultimately be fulfilled at the cross when He said, *It is finished*.

THE MENORAH DECLARED THAT JESUS WAS COMING

Therefore, the Menorah, which was one of the primary symbols of the Old Testament, was placed in the Tabernacle to declare that Jesus was coming in the flesh to deliver us by accomplishing the Finished Works of Christ. It declared the 7 days of the Perfect Creation and the perfect works that were lost, that Jesus came to win back. God's perfect works were lost by man, and then Jesus came in the flesh to bring God's perfect works back to the creation the "second time," but this time, it was with His own blood.

When Jesus accomplished His Finished Works on the cross, the veil was torn, and the way into the Most Holy Place (where the Ark was kept) was made available to all. In other words, the "Finished Works of Christ" made "Redemption" available to all. Therefore, the Menorah and the Ark line up directly with the 3rd Measure, Redemption, to reveal the Kingdom of God that we have now been invited into through the Staircase, Jesus Christ.

3 Measures of God's Plan of Redemption

1st Measure	2nd Measure	3rd Measure
"Perfect Creation" ➡	"Fall of Man" ➡	"Redemption"
1 2 3 4 5 6 **7**	1 2 3 4 5 6/gap/ **7**	1 2 3 4 5 6 7 [8]

ARK

"Kingdom of God"

CHAPTER 11

THE MENORAH AND THE NUMBER "4"

We have seen how the Menorah represents the Finished Works of Christ, and now we will look further into the Menorah as we look at the specific number associated with it. The Menorah "stands" on one central candlestick holding the 4th lamp. So the entire structure of the Menorah is not only centered around the number 4, but it is also based on it.

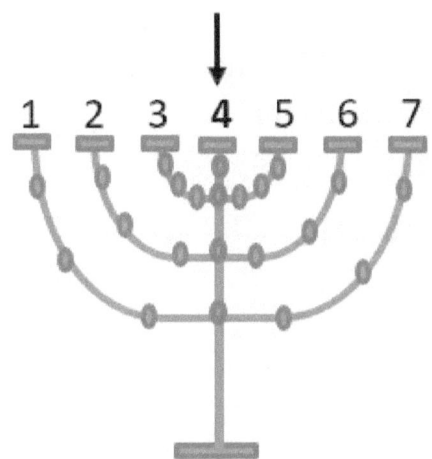

Why is the number 4 the focal point of the Menorah? It is because the Menorah represents the Finished Works of Christ, and God used the number 4 to declare that "Jesus would come in the flesh" to accomplish the works that the Father had sent him to finish.

This meaning of the number 4 can be found by following the same pattern in which we discovered the meaning of the numbers 1, 6, and 7. The meaning of each number is determined by what God did on that specific day of creation.

Following that same pattern of understanding, what did God do on the 4th day? On the 4th day, God created the sun, moon, and stars. Now ask yourself, "What was the primary creation of the 4th day?" The primary creation of the 4th day is the sun.

In Malachi 4:2, God used the "sun" to represent Jesus:

> "But to you who fear My name The Sun of
> Righteousness shall arise with healing in His
> wings...." (Malachi 4:2 NKJV)

Since the sun was created on the 4th day, and God used the sun in this scripture to represent Jesus, we know that the number 4 has something to do with Jesus. But what does the usage of the sun specifically declare about Him?

THE LIGHT OF THE SUN CAN BE SEEN WITH THE PHYSICAL EYE

You'll remember that it was on the 1st day of creation that God said, *Let there be light* and there was light. Yet "the light of the sun" was not created until the 4th day. So, there was a difference between God's light from the 1st day, and the light of the sun from the 4th day.

God's light from the 1st day is the light of His Presence that went out of man's heart after man sinned, whereas the light from the 4th day is the light of the sun that could still be seen by fallen man in the physical world. God's light that was spoken into the creation on the 1st day is "invisible" to our human physical eyes in this fallen world, yet the light of the sun, which was created on the 4th day, can still be seen by our human physical eyes in this fallen world.

THE "SUN" SERVES AS A TESTIMONY OF JESUS

Therefore, the sun (which was created on the 4th day) serves as a testimony of the light that can "still be seen" in this fallen world. The sun testifies to the fact that Jesus (who is the light) would come in the flesh to be "seen" of men and give every man the opportunity to be saved. Just as fallen man can still see the sunlight, so fallen man could also see Jesus when He came in the flesh.

So, the light of the sun that was made on the 4th day was God's witness that He would send His Son Jesus "in the flesh," who is the true light of God, to be physically manifested for all to see. He is the light of God that could be seen in this physical realm. As 1st Timothy 3:16 says, "...God was manifested in the flesh" (NKJV), and John 3:19 says, "...that the light has come into the world" (NKJV).

Not only is He the light that could be seen in the physical

realm, but He also paid the price for our sins so that we could have God's light shining in our hearts once again. In the book of 2nd Corinthians, the Apostle Paul refers to the light from the 1st day of creation, and then speaks of how God has made His light shine in our hearts through Jesus Christ.

> "For God, who commanded light to shine out of
> darkness, hath shined in our hearts, to give
> the light of the knowledge of the glory of
> God in the face of Jesus Christ." (2nd
> Corinthians 4:6 KJV)

The light (of His Presence) from the first day was lost by man, but God sent Jesus in the flesh to shine the light of His Presence in our hearts again. So, the number 4 declares that "Jesus would come in the flesh."

THE MOON AND STARS GIVE THE SAME MESSAGE

Though the sun is the primary creation of the 4th day, the moon and stars (which were also created on the 4th day) give the same message. They, too, are a witness of the light that could still be seen in the flesh (physical realm) even after God's light from the 1st day went out of man's heart. So, the moon and stars are also used to give us the same witness that Jesus would come in the flesh, for He is the true light of God that could still be seen in this fallen world or physical realm.

When you apply the meaning of the number 4 to the Menorah, the gospel message is clearly portrayed. Since the Menorah represents the Finished Works of Christ, by basing the

Menorah on the number 4, God declared that Jesus would come in the flesh to accomplish the Finished Works of Christ so that Redemption would be available to all who believe.

EXAMPLES OF THE NUMBER 4 IN THE BIBLE

Now let's look further at how God used the number 4 to declare that Jesus would come in the flesh. There are many examples in the Bible, but here is a list of five. Some of these examples are based on the number 4 itself, and others are based on what was created on the 4th day (the sun, moon, and stars).

Example 1: The Vision in Revelation 12

In the Book of Revelation, chapter 12, God gave John a vision in which He used the sun, moon, and stars (which were all created on the 4th day) to declare that Jesus would come in the flesh.

"And there appeared a great wonder in heaven; a woman clothed with the sun, and the moon under her feet, and upon her head a crown of twelve stars: And she being with child cried, travailing in birth, and pained to be delivered" (Revelation 12:1-2 KJV).

The vision goes on to say that this woman gave birth to a child that was to rule all nations with a rod of iron (Revelation 12:5). In this vision, the woman represents Israel, and the child represents Jesus. The woman was clothed with the "sun," and the "moon" was under her feet, and she had a crown of 12 "stars."

So, God used the things that were created on the 4th Day (the sun, moon, and stars) to portray the birth of Jesus in this vision, and to describe how Jesus would come in the flesh through the nation of Israel. This is a prime example of how God used the things created on the 4th day to declare that Jesus (the light of the world) would come in the flesh.

Example 2: A Star Announced the Birth of Jesus

Stars give the same message as the sun in that they declare the light that can be seen with the physical eyes, yet stars were used to give witness of the light in the night. They gave witness that Jesus, the light, would come in the flesh amid the darkness of this world, and so God used a star to announce the birth of Jesus to the wise men,

"...and behold, the star which they had seen in the East went before them, till it came and stood over where the young Child was." (Matthew 2:9 NKJV)

Here again, that which was created on the 4th day (a star) was used to declare the birth of Jesus and how He would come in the flesh.

On that same line of thought, it is no wonder that Jesus is called "the Bright and Morning Star" (Revelation 22:16 NKJV). Also, in the Old Testament, when God gave a prophecy to Balaam that Jesus would come in the flesh, He used a "star" to describe this:

"I shall see him, but not now: I shall behold him, but not nigh: there shall come a Star out of Jacob...." (Numbers 24:17 KJV)

Example 3: The Veil was Made Up of 4 Parts

"Therefore, brethren, having boldness to enter the Holiest by the blood of Jesus, by a new and living way which He consecrated for us, through the veil, that is, His flesh." (Hebrews 10:19-20 NKJV)

This scripture plainly tells us that the veil, which stood before the Most Holy Place in the Tabernacle, represents Jesus's flesh. Since the veil represents that Jesus would come in the flesh, it is easy to see why God would attach the number 4 to it.

This veil was made up of exactly 4 parts: blue, purple, scarlet, and fine twined linen (Exodus 26:31). Also, it hung on 4 pillars that stood on 4 sockets. So not only does the Bible tell us that this veil represents Jesus's flesh, but He also directly connected the number 4 to this veil in several ways, from the number of materials it was made of, to the number of sockets and pillars it stood on. Again, God used the number 4 to declare that Jesus would come in the flesh.

Example 4: The Tribe of Judah

When Jesus came in the flesh, God chose the lineage of the Messiah to be from the Tribe of Judah. Judah was Jacob's 4th son, and so Judah is the 4th tribe of Israel. Jesus is even called the Lion of the Tribe of Judah. So, God attached the number 4 to the lineage of the tribe from which Jesus would be born. Here again, we see how God used the number 4 to declare that Jesus would come in the flesh.

Example 5: The Four Gospels

There are 4 Gospels: Matthew, Mark, Luke, and John. When you understand that God uses the number 4 throughout the Bible to declare that Jesus would come in the flesh to save us, it is no wonder that God chose the specific number of "4" Gospels for the written testimony of His Son.

All five of these examples show how God used the number 4, and the things that were created on the 4th day, to declare that Jesus would come in the flesh. The Menorah declares the Finished Works of Christ, and the number 4 declares that He would come in the flesh to accomplish those works. Once we understand the meaning of the number 4, it is easy to see why God would make the entire structure of the Menorah to be centered around this number.

GOD'S PURPOSE FOR THE SYMBOLS THAT HE GAVE TO US

Why did God give us symbols like the Menorah and the Ark that line up directly with the 3rd Measure, Redemption? Because He desired to give us visible symbols and patterns in the physical realm that would help us understand the Kingdom of God that we cannot see. These two pieces of furniture stood in the Tabernacle as testimonies of all that Jesus was coming to accomplish and make available to us.

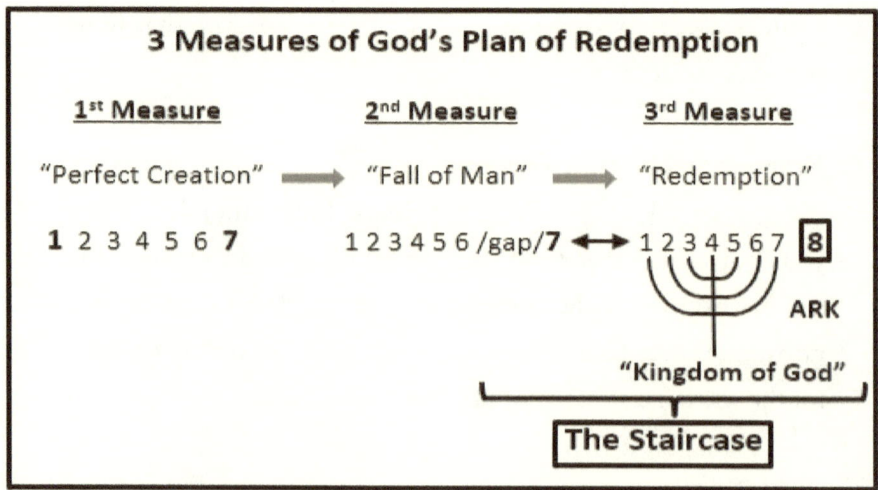

These symbols that could be seen in the physical realm served as a physical "map" of our Redemption in Christ. Here again, the entire Old Testament comes together to tell the exact same message of how Jesus, the Staircase, has made the unseen, invisible, all-powerful Kingdom of God available to those who believe.

CHAPTER 12

THE JOURNEY OF ISRAEL "MAP"

WE HAVE SEEN HOW THE MENORAH AND THE ARK served as a "map" of our Redemption in Christ that reveals the Kingdom of God that has been made available to us through Jesus. Just as the Menorah and the Ark served as a "map" of our Redemption, another "map" in the Old Testament also lines up directly with the 3 Measures of God's Plan of Redemption.

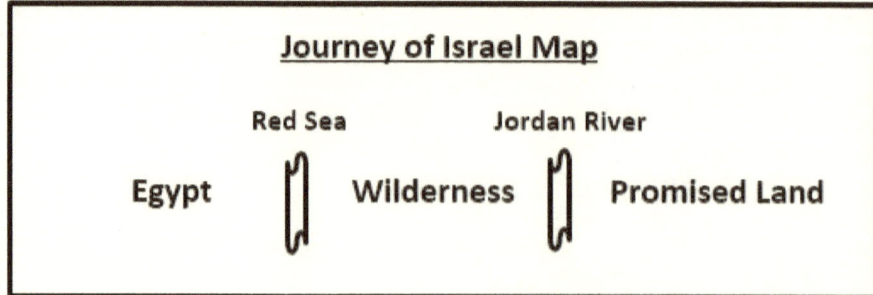

The Journey of Israel from Egypt, through the Wilderness, and into the Promised Land was one of the major events in the Old Testament, and this entire journey lays upon the same structure of the 3 Measures. The Journey of Israel was like a "map" of our Redemption that depicts every Christian's journey from the bondage of sin and death to Redemption through Jesus Christ.

In the following few chapters, we will be looking at how this journey fits directly into the structure of the 3 Measures of God's Plan of Redemption, and how God used this journey of Israel to declare the Kingdom of God that has now been freely given to us through the Staircase, Jesus Christ.

THE JOURNEY OF ISRAEL

This journey started when Israel was in bondage in the land of Egypt. God called Moses from a burning bush and sent him to Egypt to deliver His people. He was obedient to the call, and God instructed him to say these words to Pharaoh,

> "…The Lord God of the Hebrews has met with
> us; and now, please, let us go three days'
> journey into the wilderness, that we may
> sacrifice to the Lord our God."(Exodus 3:18
> NKJV)

After God delivered Israel from Egypt through the hand of Moses, they served God on that same Mount Sinai from which God had called Moses from the burning bush. At that time, God gave Moses the Ten Commandments and the pattern of the Tabernacle. They wandered 40 years in the Wilderness until the first generation was consumed. It was the second generation that entered the Promised Land under the leadership of Joshua.

EGYPT: THE HOUSE OF BONDAGE

In the Journey of Israel Map, Moses is a type and shadow of the true Savior Jesus Christ, who came to deliver us from the bondage of the world. Several times in the Bible, Egypt is called "the house of bondage." So, in the Journey of Israel Map, God used Egypt to represent the bondage of sin and this world that Jesus would come to deliver us out of.

Now let's look at how Egypt fits into the map of the "3 Measures of God's Plan of Redemption". Where would Egypt, the house of bondage, be found in the 3 Measures? We know that it would not be found in the 1st Measure because the 1st Measure is the Perfect Creation, and there was certainly no bondage or sin in God's Perfect Creation. So where is Egypt (the house of bondage) found?

It is found in the 2nd Measure, which is the Fall of Man. Egypt represents the fallen world that fell into the curse, darkness, sin, and death. It specifically represents the 6 days of creation that were separated from God's Rest, which are found in the 2nd Measure (the Fall of Man), as shown in the following illustration.

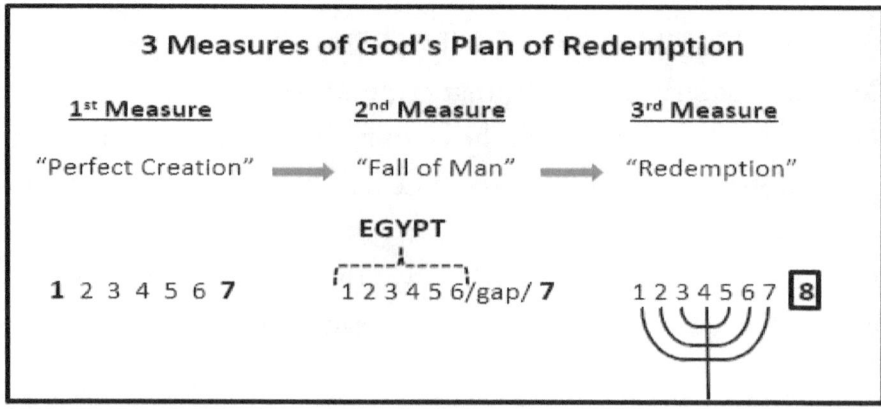

WHERE IS THE PROMISED LAND FOUND IN THE 3 MEASURES?

We have identified Egypt in the 3 Measures of God's Plan of Redemption. Now let's identify the "Promised Land." You'll remember that once man had sinned, the whole creation was separated from God's 7th-day Rest. In Psalm 95, and the book of Hebrews (chapters 3 and 4), the Bible associates God's 7th-day Rest with the Promised Land.

So, the Promised Land represents the 7th-day Rest which is found in the 2nd Measure (the Fall of Man). In the following illustration, I am using the initials "PL" for the Promised Land and am placing those initials in the position of the 7th-day Rest, for they are the same.

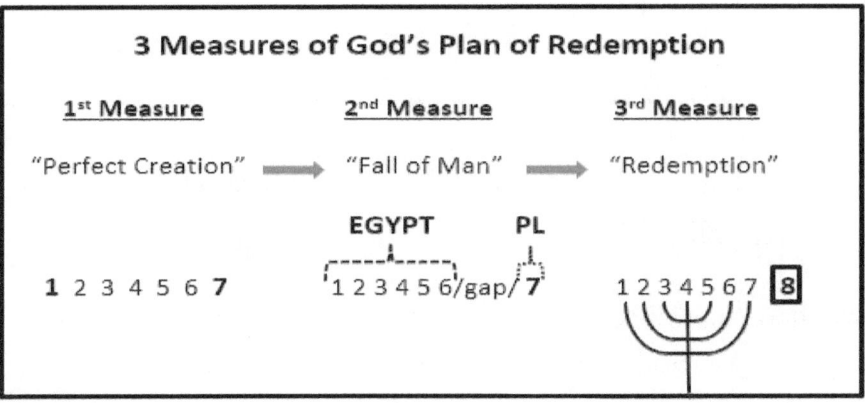

THE "7TH DAY" OF THE 2ND MEASURE

In comparing the 3 Measures to the Journey of Israel Map, it is important to understand that the "7th day" of the 2nd Measure (which man had been separated from) is synonymous with "all 7 days" of the 3rd Measure, which are represented by the Menorah.

Once Jesus entered back into that Rest for us through His own blood (which is depicted by the 7th day of the 2nd Measure), He made His Rest available to "all" 7 days of creation again.

So, in the following illustration, I am also labeling the 3rd Measure of 7 days as the "Promised Land" to declare that "all 7 days" of the 3rd Measure are synonymous with the "7th day" of the 2nd Measure.

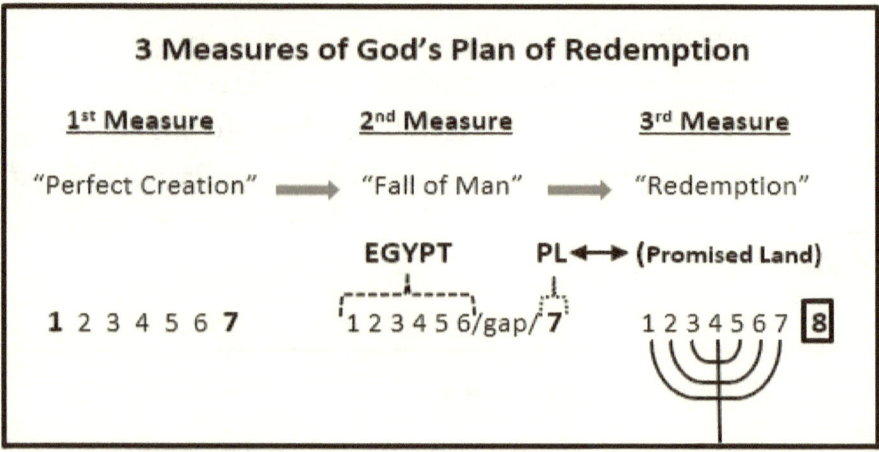

WHERE IS THE WILDERNESS FOUND IN THE 3 MEASURES?

We have identified Egypt and the Promised Land on the 3 Measures of God's Plan of Redemption. Now let's identify the "Wilderness." Since Egypt represents the fallen world, and the Promised Land represents our entrance back into God's Rest, what does God use to represent the "/gap/" which separates the fallen world from God's Rest?

God used the Wilderness to represent the "/gap/" which had to be crossed to get to the Promised Land Rest. In other words, it was this "/gap/" that had to be crossed to get to the Kingdom of God. I'm using the letter "W" to represent the Wilderness and am placing it in the position of the "/gap/" on the 3 Measures of God's Plan of Redemption Map. For in the patterns of the Lord, the "/gap/" and the Wilderness are the same.

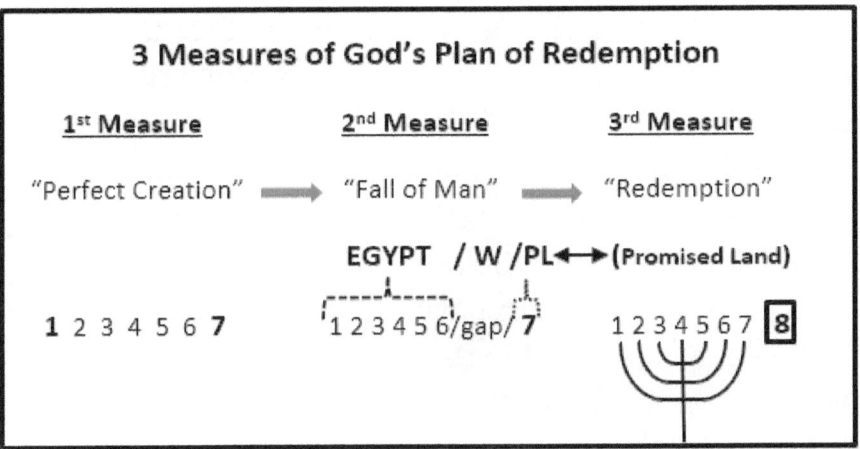

THE RED SEA AND THE JORDAN RIVER

In the journey of Israel from Egypt, through the Wilderness, and into the Promised Land, there are two natural boundary markers that God used to designate the Wilderness. The Red Sea was used as a natural boundary marker that designates the Children of Israel's entrance into the Wilderness after being delivered from Egypt. So also, the Jordan River is used as a natural boundary marker that designates their departure out of the Wilderness, and their entrance into the Promised Land.

THE RED SEA AND JORDAN RIVER ARE BOTH SYMBOLS OF BAPTISM IN CHRIST

The Red Sea and the Jordan River are both used as boundary markers to identify the Wilderness and serve as symbols of baptism in Christ. In 1st Corinthians 10, while referring to the

Red Sea, Paul explains how the Children of Israel were "baptized" unto Moses in the cloud and the (Red) Sea. This served as a symbol of the greater picture that foreshadowed how we would be baptized in Christ.

Then, Jesus was baptized in the Jordan River by John the Baptist, and His baptism in the Jordan declared all that He would accomplish at the cross. So, both the Red Sea and the Jordan are used to represent baptism in Christ.

Therefore, the Wilderness is surrounded by two boundary markers representing baptism, for it is only through baptism in Christ that we can cross this Wilderness to get to the Promised Land Rest (Kingdom of God). In the following illustration, the lines on either side of the Wilderness represent the Red Sea and the Jordan River.

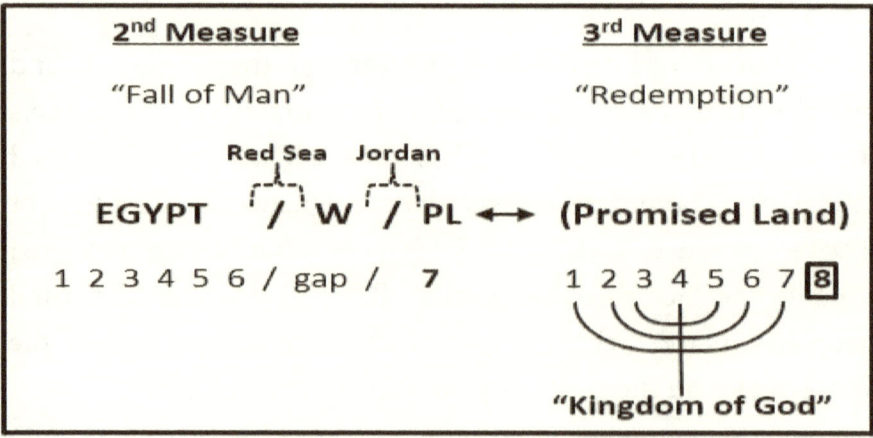

In combining the "Journey of Israel" with the "3 Measures of God's Plan of Redemption", it becomes evident that God used the entire Journey of His people Israel to be a map of our Redemption that reveals the Kingdom of God.

God used Egypt to represent the fallen world and the bondage of sin. He used the Wilderness to represent the immense "/gap/" that stood between God and His creation because of sin. He used the Promised Land to represent the unseen, invisible, all-powerful Kingdom of God that is now available to all who believe in Jesus.

CHAPTER 13

THE WILDERNESS DESCRIBES THE "/GAP/"

In the Journey of Israel Map, we have seen how the Wilderness represents the "/gap/" that stood between God and His creation. It was in this region of the Wilderness that God gave us several types and shadows to illustrate further the immense "/gap/" that stood between God and man because of sin, and also to provide us with a greater understanding of how no one could cross this "/gap/" to reach the Kingdom of God except Jesus.

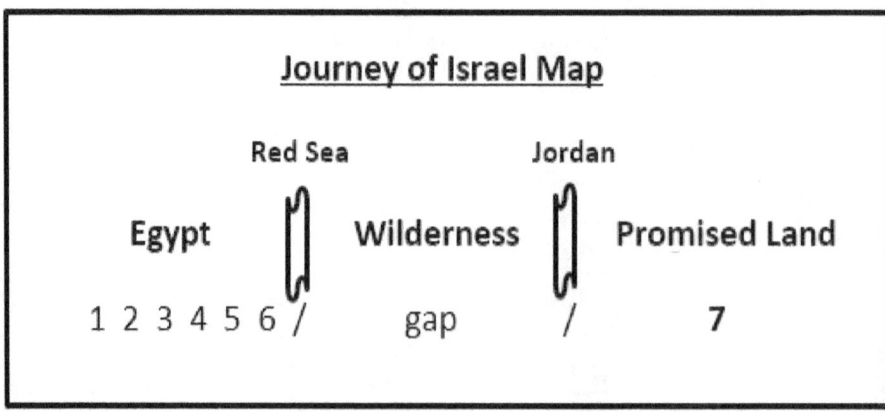

TEN COMMANDMENTS WERE GIVEN IN THE WILDERNESS

It was in this region of the Wilderness that they came to Mount Sinai, where God gave the Ten Commandments to Moses. The New Testament tells us that the Law was given to point out our sin, and to show us our need for the Savior. It was our schoolmaster that leads us to Christ (Galatians 3:24 KJV).

The Ten Commandments literally identified this "/gap/" of sin that stood between God and man and declared the region that our flesh could never cross except through Jesus. So, the Ten Commandments (which were given in the Wilderness) were used to define the price that had to be paid before the "/gap/" could be crossed. They were used to point us to Jesus, the Staircase, who bridged the "/gap/" and made it possible for us to get back to the Father.

THE TABERNACLE WAS MADE IN THE WILDERNESS

It was also in this region called the Wilderness (upon Mount Sinai) that God gave Moses the pattern of the Tabernacle. God used this Tabernacle to give us further understanding of the "/gap/" that stood between God and man. The Tabernacle was a physical building that served as a pattern or copy of the true heavenly things that we cannot see.

> "For Christ has not entered the holy places made
> with hands, which are copies of the true, but
> into heaven itself, now to appear in the

presence of God for us." (Hebrews 9:24
NKJV)

Even though we cannot see the spirit realm, God revealed His
Kingdom by giving us these visible symbols in the physical realm.
As mentioned in the verse above, these *copies of the true,* were
examples of the true heavenly things themselves. He did this to
help us lay hold of the meaning of those things that we cannot
see, and to help us understand that the Kingdom was "not yet
available" until Jesus came.

Remember that a veil stood before the Holy of Holies (where
the Ark was placed) to show that the way into the Holiest of All
was not accessible until Jesus. In other words, through the
Tabernacle that was given in the Wilderness, He was showing us
that the "/gap/" could not be crossed until Jesus came to cross it
for us.

MOUNT SINAI WAS ALSO IN THE "WILDERNESS"

In this same region of the Wilderness, God also used Mount Sinai
to further identify and teach us about the immense "/gap/" that
stood between God and man. Several times in the Bible, a
mountain is used to represent a kingdom. God used Mount Sinai
(in the Wilderness) to represent the Kingdom of God, and to
show how the Kingdom of God was not accessible until Jesus
came to make it accessible to us.

Before we continue looking at how Mount Sinai represents
the Kingdom of God, and how it was used to illustrate further
the "/gap/" that stood between God and man, it is important to

establish the meaning of a number that God used in connection with this mountain, which is the Number "12".

THE NUMBER 12 REPRESENTS THE KINGDOM OF GOD

The number 12 is the number for the government and authority which is above all other governments and authorities, for it is the number of the Kingdom of God. Think about this, God used 12 tribes to declare His Kingdom in the Old Testament, and 12 disciples to declare His Kingdom in the New Testament. When the soldiers came for Jesus in the Garden, Jesus used the number 12 in describing the authority and power of His Kingdom when He said,

> "Or do you think that I cannot now pray to My
> Father, and He will provide Me with more
> than twelve legions of angels?" (Matthew
> 26:53 NKJV)

Also, in the vision of Revelation 12:1, God used a crown of 12 stars on the woman's head to represent His Kingdom. In this revelation, God directly associated the number 12 with a "crown," representing His Kingdom, and how the Kingdom of God would be made available through Jesus.

The number 12 is also shown as the number of His Kingdom in the 21st chapter of the Book of Revelation. In this chapter, God used the number 12 in many ways to describe the Holy Jerusalem, which is a picture of the Kingdom of God being established in fullness on this earth.

It is important to understand that God uses the number 12 in scripture to represent the Kingdom of God because God used this exact number at the base of Mount Sinai. Moses set up 12 pillars at the foot of the mountain according to the 12 tribes of Israel (Exodus 24:4). In using the number 12 at the base of this mountain, God was giving us a confirmation of how this Mount Sinai in the Wilderness represented the Kingdom of God.

NOT ACCESSIBLE UNTIL JESUS

They were told not to touch this mountain (which represented the Kingdom of God), and they were also told to sanctify themselves "today and tomorrow," and on "the third day," at the sound of a trumpet, the Lord came down on the mountain in fire. At that time, all the assembly was to gather at the Mount as God spoke the Ten Commandments to them. Moses stood between them and the Lord at that time, and they gained the understanding of how they needed Moses to be their intercessor.

Notice how a total of "3 days" were mentioned. Those 3 days served as a symbol of the greater picture of how Jesus would die for our sins on the 1st day, His body would lay in the grave on the entire 2nd Day (the Sabbath Day), and how He would rise from the grave on the 3rd Day, so that we could be saved and have access to the Kingdom.

God was using this to teach us that there was no access to the Kingdom of God (which was represented by Mount Sinai) until Jesus came. In other words, there was no way to get across the "/gap/" until the Staircase appeared.

DON'T TOUCH THE MOUNTAIN

Remember that they were told not to touch the mountain. The Bible says,

> "You shall set bounds for the people all around,
>   saying, 'Take heed to yourselves that you do
>   not go up to the mountain or touch its base.
>   Whoever touches the mountain shall surely
>   be put to death.'" (Exodus 19:12 NKJV)

Just as they were told not to touch the mountain, the New Testament says that "flesh and blood cannot inherit the Kingdom of God" (1st Corinthians 15:50). For it is only through the blood of Jesus that we have access to the Kingdom of God.

In the book of Hebrews 12:18-24, the Bible makes a clear comparison and distinction between Mount Sinai, which they were not supposed to touch, and the Kingdom of God, which is now freely made available to us through Jesus. So, God used Mount Sinai to declare that His Kingdom was not accessible until Jesus came to pay the price for our sins.

Therefore, in the region of the Wilderness, whether it was the Ten Commandments, the Tabernacle, or Mount Sinai, God was revealing the "/gap/" which stood between God and man.

The Ten Commandments declared the price that would have to be paid to get to the Kingdom of God. The Tabernacle was the pattern of heavenly things that showed how the way into the Holiest of All (the Kingdom of God) was not yet manifest while the first Tabernacle was still standing. Mount Sinai also declared that the Kingdom of God was unavailable until Jesus came to pay the price for it.

Through all these signs in the Wilderness, He was showing us that the only way to get across this "/gap/" and into the Kingdom of God is through Jesus, the Staircase. Now we will look further into this Wilderness as we look at the one specific number that God associated with it, which is the number "40."

CHAPTER 14

THE NUMBER "40"

We have seen how God used the Wilderness in many ways to describe the "/gap/" that stood between God and His creation because of sin. There is also one specific number that God associated with both the Wilderness and the "/gap/," and that number is 40. God used the number 40 many times in the Bible, and when a number is consistently mentioned in the Bible, it should always get our attention as to why.

It rained for 40 days in the account of Noah's ark. Isaac was 40 years old when he took Rebekah to be his wife. After the death of Jacob, Joseph commanded his servants to embalm his father, Israel, for 40 days. Moses fasted for 40 days on Mount Sinai. The twelve spies searched out the Promised Land for 40 days. The Children of Israel wandered for 40 years in the Wilderness until the first generation died. God also fed the Children of Israel with manna for 40 years in that same Wilderness.

Goliath withstood Israel for 40 days. King David reigned for 40 years. King David's son, Solomon, reigned for 40 years as well.

Elijah traveled for 40 days to get to the Mount of God. The Lord instructed Jonah to give Nineveh the time of 40 days to repent.

Mary waited 40 days after Jesus was born before she presented Him at the Temple, as was prescribed by the law of Moses regarding the days of purification. Jesus fasted for 40 days in the Wilderness of Judah before returning in the power of the Spirit. He also showed Himself alive for 40 days after He was resurrected and spoke to them of things pertaining to the Kingdom of God.

Since the number 40 was used so many times, it is evident that this number is very important to God, so a specific message must be attached to it. What does God want us to see about the number 40? Its meaning can be found in the way that God directly associated this number with the Wilderness.

GOD MARKED THE WILDERNESS WITH THE NUMBER 40

In the Book of Numbers 14:32-34, God directly associated the number 40 with the Wilderness when He caused the Children of Israel to wander for 40 years until the first generation died. So, in the journey of Israel, the entire Wilderness experience was "marked" by the number 40.

We have already seen, in the Journey of Israel, how the Wilderness represents the "/gap/." So, the number 40 would then represent both the Wilderness and the "/gap/," and they are, therefore, all three synonymous with one another.

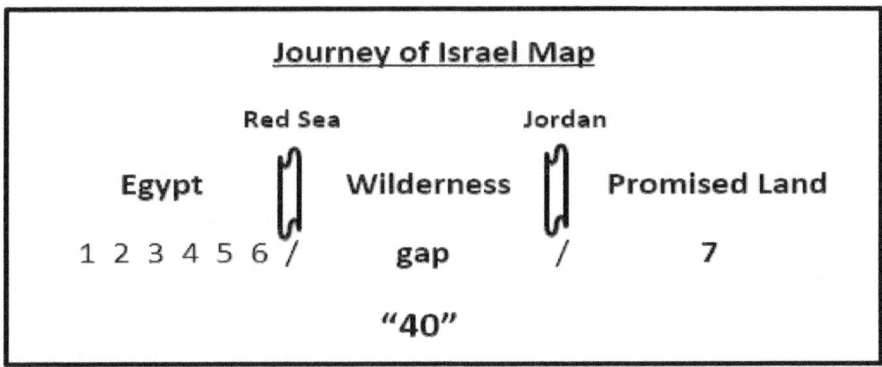

Whether it was 40 days of rain, the 40 days that Goliath withstood Israel, or Jesus's 40-day fast, God was constantly speaking to us about the "/gap/" that stood between God and man because of sin.

THE NUMBER 40 DECLARES THE PROBLEM AND THE ANSWER

The number 40 not only identifies the "/gap/" that we could not cross, but it also speaks of the only man that could cross it, Jesus Christ. He is the perfect lamb, the perfect Son of God, and the only man that could cross that "/gap/" and walk in God's Promised Land Rest which is the Kingdom of God.

So, God first used the number 40 to declare the immense "/gap/" of sin that stood between God and His creation, and that same number also declares the answer to the problem. In other words, the number 40 declared the problem so that God could point us to the solution.

EXAMPLE OF DAVID AND GOLIATH

The account of David and Goliath gives us a perfect example of how the number 40 not only identifies the problem, but also declares the answer. Israel's problem was Goliath, who withstood them for 40 days, but then God brought the answer to that problem when He sent David to win the battle.

Goliath was a type and shadow of the sin keeping us from God. The "40 days" in which Goliath withstood Israel, represents the "/gap/" between God and His creation because of sin. David was a type and shadow of our Savior Jesus, who defeated sin for us, and made it possible for us to cross the "/gap/" and walk in the Kingdom of God.

Just as David was God's answer to Goliath withstanding his people for 40 days, Jesus is God's answer to the sin that was keeping us from God and His Kingdom. So, the number 40 both identified the problem and declared the answer, Jesus Christ, the Staircase who bridged the "/gap/" so that we could cross over from this fallen world into the Kingdom of God.

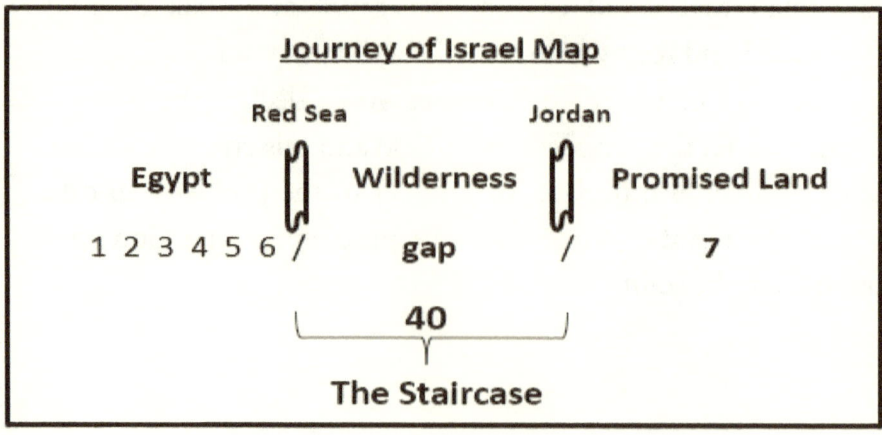

40 ALSO REPRESENTS THE "DEATH OF OUR FLESH IN CHRIST"

The number 40 not only declares the "/gap/" that no one could cross except Jesus, but it also declares that the only way for us to get across the "/gap/" is for our flesh to be "dead in Christ." Once we have received Jesus as our Savior, the Bible tells us that something specifically happens to our spirit, and something specifically happens to our flesh.

Our spirit is made "alive" in Christ, while our flesh "dies" in Christ. The number 40 is the number that God uses to declare that specific part of our salvation that has to do with our flesh, for it declares the death of our flesh in Christ. In order for us to cross that "/gap/" and walk in the Kingdom of God, our flesh has to be dead in Christ.

The first time that we see the number 40 in the Bible was in the account of Noah's Ark when God caused it to rain 40 days and nights until all flesh "died" except for the 8 people and the animals on the Ark. So, the first time that we see the number 40 in the Bible it was associated with death. Why death? Because God was speaking to us about the "death of our flesh in Christ."

In 1st Peter 3:18-22, the New Testament reveals that the account of Noah's ark served as a symbol of water baptism in Christ. What happens when we are baptized in Christ? When we are baptized in Christ, our flesh goes under the water in the likeness of His death, and then we are raised up out of the water in the likeness of His resurrection.

In Romans 6:3, Paul made the point that we are baptized into His death. So, the 40 days of rain in the account of Noah's ark would then declare that part of baptism in which our flesh goes under the water in the likeness of His "death."

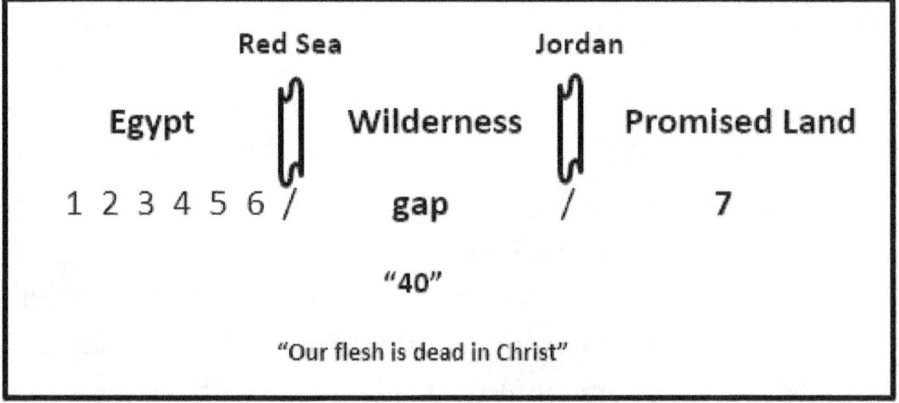

THE MESSAGE OF THE FIRST AND SECOND GENERATION

This understanding of how the number 40 represents the "death of our flesh in Christ," also comes from the way that God directly associated the number 40 with the death of the "first generation" in the Wilderness. What happened to the Children of Israel during those 40 years in the Wilderness? They wandered for 40 years until the first generation "died." So, the number 40 is directly connected with the death of the first generation. Why death? Because God used the first generation to declare that our flesh has to die in Christ.

So, it was the first generation that died in the Wilderness after wandering for 40 years, and it was the second generation that entered the Promised Land. The death of the first generation is directly associated with the Wilderness, the "/gap/," and the number 40, while the second generation is directly associated with the Promised Land Rest. What is God telling us with this message of the first and second generations?

Think about this for a moment. How were we "first" born into this world? We were born first "in the flesh." How are we born again? We are born the second time (born again) "in the Spirit." Now compare this to the first and second generations.

Just as the first generation had to die in the Wilderness, so also, the first way that we are born into this world (the flesh) has to die in Christ. And just as the second generation entered the Promised Land, so also, it is the second way that we are born (when we are born of the Spirit), that we enter the Promised Land Rest, which is the Kingdom of God.

So, the first generation and second generation represented what happens to us as we become Christians. Just as Paul described in Romans 8:10,

> "And if Christ is in you, then the body is dead
> because of sin, but the Spirit is life because of
> righteousness." (NKJV)

Also, in Colossians 3:3,

> "For you died, and your life is hidden with Christ
> in God." (NKJV)

When he says, "For you died," he is specifically describing what happens to our flesh as we become a Christian, for our flesh dies in Christ. In other words, the only way for us to cross the "/gap/" (or Wilderness), is for our flesh to be dead in Christ. Therefore, God directly associated the number 40 with the death of the first generation because God was giving us the message that our flesh must die in Christ in order for us to enter the Kingdom of God.

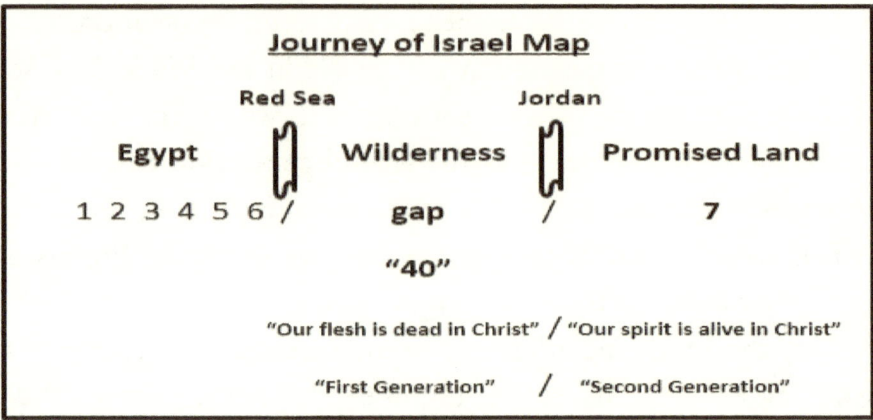

40 ALSO DECLARES THE REMAINDER OF OUR JOURNEY

Since the number 40 declares the death of our flesh in Christ, it also declares the remainder of our journey on this earth as Christians. Even though our flesh dies in Christ when we become Christians, we are not immediately raptured up to Heaven. No, we still remain on this earth.

Think about this. When we receive Jesus as our Savior, our flesh becomes "dead in Christ." Yet we are living out the remainder of our days on this earth in our physical bodies as we are still in this fallen world. Though we are dead in Christ, we are still told to put the deeds of the flesh to death daily by walking in the spirit.

So, the number 40 not only represents the "/gap/" that could only be crossed through the death of our flesh in Jesus Christ, but it also represents the remainder of our journey of faith on this earth as Christians while we are still in the body.

JESUS SHOWED HIMSELF ALIVE FOR 40 DAYS

We have seen how the number 40 represents the "death of our flesh in Christ." Yet in Acts 1:3, the Bible says that Jesus showed Himself "alive" for 40 days. Now why would Jesus show Himself alive for an exact number that is used to represent death? It was to declare His total victory over death and how He ever lives to make intercession for us as we are still journeying through this earth.

Jesus died for our sins once, and now "He lives" forevermore. So, when we receive Jesus as our Savior, our flesh becomes "dead" in Christ, who is "alive." In other words, we immediately cross that Wilderness in Christ because He has already crossed it for us, and our flesh is considered "dead" in Christ. Yet the Wilderness also still signifies the remainder of our journey on this earth as Christians because we are still in the body.

When Jesus showed Himself "alive" for 40 days, He was declaring that He is our intercessor in this time of the Wilderness, which still represents the remainder of our journey of faith on this earth as a Christian. Every physical need and trial that we face as Christians on this earth is primarily represented by the Wilderness, and He showed Himself alive for 40 days to declare that He is more than enough to help us through any trial or tribulation that we will ever face.

He is our High Priest who constantly makes intercession for us. He is our deliverer who is ready to help us every day. Just as Jesus said,

"...In the world you will have tribulation; but be
of good cheer, I have overcome the world."
(John 16:33 NKJV)

Therefore, in all the times that God used the number 40, He was declaring the Wilderness or "/gap/" that no one could cross except Jesus. Then once we have received Jesus as our Savior, this number declares the death of our flesh in Christ, and the remainder of our journey of faith on this earth while we are still in the body. God used the number 40 throughout the Bible to carry this distinct message about our Redemption through the Staircase, Jesus Christ.

CHAPTER 15

BOTH THE WILDERNESS AND THE PROMISED LAND

SINCE THE ENTIRE JOURNEY OF ISRAEL IS A MAP OF OUR Redemption in Christ, it is vital for us as Christians to understand our placement on this map. Every Christian is in "both" the Wilderness and the Promised Land while we are still on this earth. Only a "non-believer" is still in Egypt.

Journey of Israel Map

{*Nonbelievers*} {   *Christians*   }

       Red Sea   **Jordan**

Egypt   〔〕   **Wilderness**   〔〕   **Promised Land**

1 2 3 4 5 6 /   gap   /   7

THE JORDAN RIVER IS THE "STARTING POINT" FOR A CHRISTIAN

Every person starts out in the bondage of Egypt. When we make a decision of faith to believe in Jesus, we instantly leave Egypt and cross the Wilderness (because Jesus has already crossed it for us) and find ourselves in the Jordan River. The Jordan River is the place where Jesus was baptized, and so the Jordan represents the death, burial, and resurrection of Jesus.

The Jordan is where Jesus began His ministry, and it is where we begin our life and journey as Christians on this map. So, the Jordan River is the "starting point" for every believer on this Journey of Israel Map, and it represents our new birth as Christians, which the Bible calls the "washing of regeneration and renewing of the Holy Spirit" (Titus 3:5 NKJV).

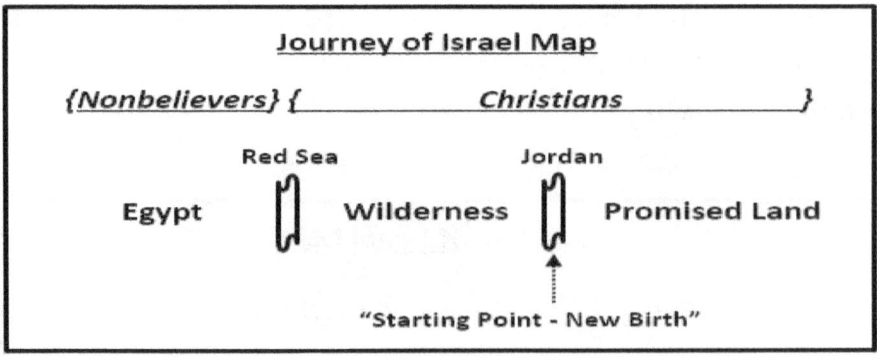

Once we have washed in the Jordan River (which is our new birth in Christ), we have immediate access to the Promised Land because Jesus has already paid the price for us to be there. The Promised Land represents the spirit realm of God (the Kingdom of God) in which we are now free to walk in, and where we can now worship the Father in spirit and truth.

Yet our flesh doesn't just go away. No, we are still in the body, still in the flesh, still in this world. We are in the world, but no longer of the world. God has placed us in a "place of separation" from this world which is called the Wilderness. Though we instantly cross the Wilderness in Christ once we have believed in Jesus, the Wilderness also still represents the remainder of our journey of faith on this earth while we are still in the body.

Both the Promised Land and the Wilderness simply describe our position as Christians. The Promised Land identifies our spirit, and the Wilderness identifies our flesh. The Promised Land represents "Our walk in the Spirit" once we have been born again, while the Wilderness represents the "death of our flesh in Christ," and the remainder of our journey of faith in this earth.

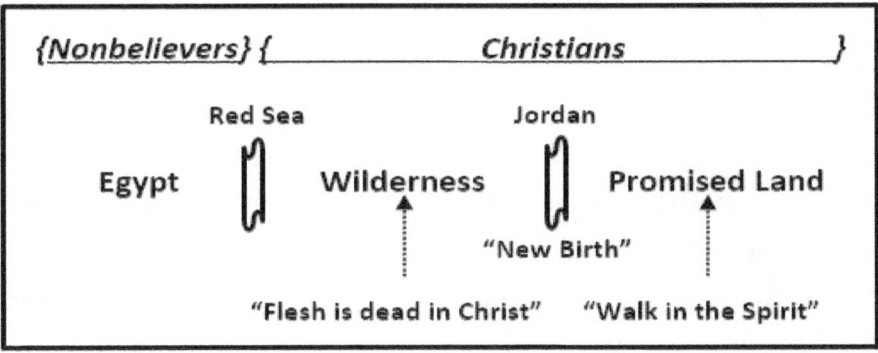

Therefore, as Christians, we are still in this fallen world that we see all around us (the Wilderness), but we are also in the Kingdom of God (the Promised Land) because the Holy Spirit dwells in us. Every Christian is in both the Promised Land and the Wilderness, while a non-believer has never made it out of "Egypt."

NONBELIEVERS ARE STILL IN EGYPT

The Bible refers to Egypt as the house of bondage. In this Journey of Israel Map, every person starts out in the bondage of Egypt, for it represents all the sin and bondage of this world that every person is born into. Only those who receive Jesus as their Savior are freed from the bondage of Egypt.

THE FIRST PASSOVER

Remember that Israel's departure from Egypt occurred on the night of the first Passover. In the Passover, all the firstborn of Egypt were killed, but the angel "passed over" all the doors which were covered by the blood of the Lamb.

The Passover was a type and shadow that would ultimately be fulfilled when Jesus came in the flesh. This was an exact picture of how all who believe in Jesus are covered by the blood of the Lamb and saved from the bondage of sin and death that is represented by Egypt.

The Children of Israel left Egypt, and the Egyptian army soon chased after them. At that time, God opened the Red Sea and made a way for all the Israelites to cross over. Then God closed the Red Sea on the Egyptians, destroying them. So, God used the Red Sea as a symbol of the greater picture of how we would be delivered from the bondage of this world through Jesus.

It was only those who took part in the Passover that crossed over the Red Sea into the wilderness with Moses. So also, only those who receive Jesus as their Savior depart from the bondage of this world and find themselves in a "place of separation" from the world called the Wilderness. Any person who hears the gospel and does not receive it is still in Egypt, for they have never departed from the bondage of this world through the blood of Jesus.

THE WILDERNESS IS A "PLACE OF SEPARATION" FOR BELIEVERS

Moses spoke to Pharaoh about the Wilderness, and his exact words were a testimony of all that Jesus would accomplish and fulfill. Moses said to Pharaoh,

> " ...let us go three days' journey into the
> wilderness, that we may sacrifice to the Lord
> our God." (Exodus 3:18 NKJV)

In this one statement, Moses spoke of *three days*, and a place of separation from Egypt called the *wilderness*. He also stated that the purpose was so that they could *sacrifice* to God.

This all served as a symbol of the greater picture of all that Jesus would fulfill, for it was in "3 days" that Jesus delivered us. On the 1st day, Jesus died for our sins. On the 2nd day, His body laid in the grave the entire Sabbath day, and on the 3rd day, He rose from the grave so that we could not only be in a place of separation from the world called the "Wilderness," but so that we could also present ourselves as a "living sacrifice" to God.

Just as the Bible describes in Romans 12:1,

> "I beseech you therefore, brethren, by the mercies
> of God, that you present your bodies a living

> sacrifice, holy, acceptable to God, which is
> your reasonable service." (NKJV)

Once we have been cleansed by the blood of Jesus, the Bible says that we can present our bodies as a living sacrifice.

Therefore, as Christians, even though we are still "in" this fallen world, God does not consider us as being "of" the world. In other words, as Christians, God no longer sees us as being in Egypt. No, we have been delivered out of Egypt and are in a place of separation called the Wilderness. Though our bodies are still in this world, God will no longer view a Christian as being in the bondage of Egypt.

He made a place of separation from the world called the Wilderness where we can now serve God as a living sacrifice, and that is where He considers our "flesh" to be on the Journey of Israel Map. We are still in this world, but not of the world.

THE WILDERNESS IS AN EXAMPLE FOR CHRISTIANS

Therefore, as Christians, the Promised Land represents how we can now walk in the Spirit (the Kingdom of God). Yet the Wilderness describes the fact that our flesh didn't just go away, but that we are still in this fallen world in a place of separation.

It is important to understand that the New Testament uses the Wilderness as an example to believers and a loving warning to exhort us to continue in the faith for the remainder of our journey on this earth while we are still in the body.

In 1st Corinthians 10:1-13, Paul used the Wilderness as an example for Christians, and in doing so, he exhorts us not to go

CHAPTER 15 | 135

astray as they had done. He described those in the Wilderness as those who drank from the Rock, and that "the Rock" represented Jesus. Then He went on to explain in verses 5 & 6,

> "But with many of them God was not well
> pleased: for they were overthrown in the
> wilderness. Now these things were our
> examples, to the intent we should not lust
> after evil things, as they also lusted." (KJV)

The Book of Hebrews (chapters 3 & 4) also speaks of those in the Wilderness, and uses those in the Wilderness as an example and loving warning to believers:

> "Beware, brethren, lest there be in any of you an
> evil heart of unbelief in departing from the
> living God; but exhort one another daily
> while it is called 'Today,' lest any of you be
> hardened through the deceitfulness of sin.
> For we have become partakers of Christ if we
> hold the beginning of our confidence
> steadfast to the end." (Hebrews 3:12-14
> NKJV)

This is another loving warning to us as Christians so that we might know the importance of keeping the faith to the end. The author of Hebrews is telling us that while it is called "Today" (while we are still on our journey as Christians on this earth), we should exhort one another daily, lest any of us go astray by returning to a lifestyle of sin. He then goes on to say that we are made partakers of Christ "if" we continue till the end.

Just as Paul gave testimony at the end of his own life of how he had kept the faith when he said, "I have fought the good fight, I have finished the race, I have kept the faith" (2nd Timothy 4:7 NKJV).

BREAD IN THE WILDERNESS

The bread that was given to Israel in the Wilderness was also used to declare this same point of how we should keep our focus on Jesus for the remainder of our journey on this earth. God fed the Children of Israel with manna (or bread) from Heaven for 40 years in the Wilderness. In the Gospel of John, Jesus identified Himself as that bread from Heaven when He said,

> "...Most assuredly, I say to you, Moses did not
> give you the bread from heaven, but My
> Father gives you the true bread from heaven.
> For the bread of God is He who comes down
> from heaven and gives life to the world."
> (John 6:32-33 NKJV)

Jesus was explaining how the manna from Heaven that was given for 40 years in the Wilderness represented Himself and how He is the "true" bread from Heaven. The message of the Wilderness is clear, in the remainder of our journey on this earth as Christians, we are to constantly feed on the true bread from Heaven, Jesus Christ. We are to continue in faith to the end.

The Bible says to "Examine yourselves as to whether you are

in the faith. Test yourselves..." (2nd Corinthians 13:5 NKJV). Are we continuing to feed on the true bread from Heaven? Are we daily feeding on the Word of God, Jesus Christ, or are we turning our hearts back to Egypt? Jesus said,

> "...No one, having put his hand to the plow, and
> looking back, is fit for the Kingdom of God."
> (Luke 9:62 NKJV)

As Christians, we are in both the Promised Land and the Wilderness. Just as the 1st generation died in the Wilderness, so also, our flesh is dead in Christ. Just as the 2nd generation entered the Promised Land, so also our spirit is born again in Christ (we are born the 2nd time). Yet we are not immediately raptured up to Heaven. No, we still remain on this earth in a place of separation called the Wilderness.

For the remainder of our journey on this earth, we have a daily choice to walk in the spirit or the flesh. In other words, are we going to walk in the Promised Land or the Wilderness? By His grace and mercy through the blood of Jesus and the power of the Holy Spirit, we can always walk in the Promised Land (Kingdom of God) by simply having faith and keeping the faith.

CHAPTER 16

WALK IN THE PROMISED LAND

IN THE JOURNEY OF ISRAEL MAP, GOD'S REVELATION OF the Promised Land is our invitation to walk in the Kingdom of God. Once we have chosen the Staircase, Jesus Christ, we are born of the Spirit and can now walk in the Spirit (signified by the Promised Land). Yet we are still in these physical bodies in this world (signified by the Wilderness).

Since we take part in both, *we* have a daily choice of whether we will "walk" in the Promised Land or the Wilderness. In other words, we have a daily choice of whether we will walk in the Spirit (the Kingdom of God) or in the flesh (the ways of this world).

Why would we ever let the enemy tempt us to walk in the Wilderness (the flesh), when we have the wonderful opportunity to walk in the Promised Land and dwell in His glorious Presence? Every day the Lord is calling His people to stop wandering in the Wilderness and walk in the Promised Land.

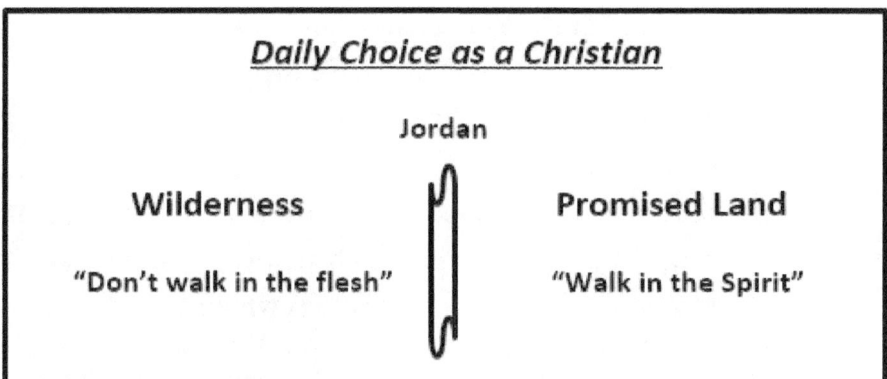

HOW DO WE "WALK" IN THE PROMISED LAND?

Remember that our walk is determined by whatever we choose to keep our mind on (Romans 8:4-6). We walk in the Promised Land by keeping our mind on things above, the things of the Spirit, by constantly feeding on the Word of God, continually being thankful to the Lord, and spending time to worship Him. By loving others as Christ has loved us, by constantly going forward in Christ and desiring His Presence and His Kingdom more than anything else in our life, and by simply holding on to His Promises and keeping the faith.

That is what it looks like to walk in the Promised Land. For when our mind is on Jesus, we are walking in the Spirit, and when we are walking in the Spirit, then we will not fulfill the lusts of the flesh (Galatians 5:16). Walking in the Promised Land is a picture of what the Christian life should look like. It is always about leaving the things of the flesh behind, pressing on, and reaching forward to what is ahead.

In Philippians 3:12-15, Paul describes the way our lives should look as Christians:

> "Not that I have already attained or am already
> perfected, but I press on, that I may lay hold
> of that for which Christ Jesus has also laid
> hold of me. Brethren, I do not count myself
> to have apprehended; but one thing I do,
> forgetting those things which are behind and
> reaching forward to those things which are
> ahead, I press toward the goal for the prize of
> the upward call of God in Christ Jesus."
> (NKJV)

In the Gospel of Luke, Jesus describes this same picture of what a Christian's life should look like when He spoke of those on the *good ground*. He explained that those on the good ground are those who,

> "...having heard the word with a noble and good
> heart, keep it and bear fruit with patience."
> (Luke 8:15 NKJV)

That is to say that a Christian's life should always have the characteristics of one who hears the Word of God and keeps it. It is a lifestyle that shows a departure from the darkness, and a fervent desire to walk in the Light of Jesus. Walking in the Promised Land is synonymous with the keeping of the faith.

DON'T WALK IN THE WILDERNESS

On the other hand, if we keep our mind on the things of the flesh, then we will walk in the flesh (which is the Wilderness).

Positionally speaking, the Wilderness represents the death of our flesh as Christians and the remainder of our journey on this earth while we are still in the body. Yet even though the Wilderness represents the remainder of our journey of faith on this earth, we still should not "walk" in the Wilderness. Instead, we should "walk" in the Promised Land.

When we walk in the Wilderness, that is the same as turning our hearts back to Egypt, back to the ways of this world, and building again those things which were destroyed at the cross (Galatians 2:17-18). Yet when we walk in the Promised Land (in the Spirit), we are putting the deeds of the flesh to death daily, and we are making our flesh line up with the position that has already been given to us in Christ (for our flesh is dead in Christ). Just as Romans 13:14 says,

> "But put on the Lord Jesus Christ, and make no provision for the flesh, to fulfill its lusts."
> (NKJV)

WALKING IN THE PROMISED LAND CAUSES HIS POWER TO FLOW

The Journey of Israel Map not only shows us our position as Christians, and how we can now walk in the Promised Land (the Kingdom of God), but it also helps us to see what the Lord will do as we walk in the Promised Land. When we walk in the Promised Land, by keeping our mind on the things of the Spirit instead of the flesh, then the Lord will cause His power to flow upon our problems in the Wilderness (physical realm).

Since the Wilderness represents the remainder of our journey on this earth as Christians, then it would also represent all the needs that we still have in the body while we remain on this earth. Every physical need that we have, such as food, shelter, and clothing, can be identified by this region of the Wilderness on the Journey of Israel Map. It is when we seek Him first by keeping our mind on the things of the Spirit that His power flows to our needs and problems in this physical realm.

TREASURE IN EARTHEN VESSELS

The Bible calls our physical body an earthen vessel and tells us that we have been given treasure in these earthen vessels. In 2nd Corinthians 4:7, Paul says,

> "But we have this treasure in earthen vessels, that
> the excellence of the power may be of God
> and not of us." (NKJV)

Paul is saying that in these *earthen vessels* (our body), we have been given the wonderful *treasure* of the Holy Spirit.

Now compare this understanding to the Journey of Israel Map. The Wilderness represents the earthen vessel (our body), while the Promised Land represents the treasure (the Holy Spirit). You see, even though we are still in this world in what the Bible calls an earthen vessel, we have been given great treasure within these earthen vessels, for we have been given the precious gift of the Holy Spirit.

. . .

```
+-----------------------------------------------------------+
|                Daily Choice as a Christian                |
|                                                           |
|                         Jordan                            |
|                                                           |
|       Wilderness            ))         Promised Land       |
|                             ))                            |
|  "Earthen Vessels (our body)"      "Treasure of the Holy Spirit" |
+-----------------------------------------------------------+
```

IT IS WHEN WE WALK IN THE PROMISED LAND THAT THE power of the Holy Spirit (the treasure) flows to our problems in the Wilderness (these earthen vessels).

EARTHEN VESSELS HAVE NEEDS

Jesus knows of our needs in these earthen vessels (our body). In Matthew 6:31-33, Jesus spoke of the needs of the body,

> "Therefore do not worry, saying 'What shall we
>   eat?' or 'What shall we drink?' or 'What shall
>   we wear?' For after all these things the
>   Gentiles seek. For your heavenly Father
>   knows that you need all these things. But seek
>   first the kingdom of God and His
>   righteousness, and all these things shall be
>   added to you." (NKJV)

Jesus was telling us to seek Him first in "spirit and truth," and then He will provide the physical things for us. Now put this together with the message of the Promised Land and the Wilderness. It is when we walk in the Promised Land by keeping our mind on the things of the Spirit that His power will flow upon the physical needs that we have in these earthen vessels in the Wilderness.

HIS WATER FLOWS TO OUR WILDERNESS

God describes the act of His power meeting our needs and problems on this earth as *waters* breaking forth in the Wilderness. In Isaiah 35:5-6, the Bible was foretelling of the healing power of God that would take place when Jesus came in the flesh:

> "Then the eyes of the blind shall be opened, and
> the ears of the deaf shall be unstopped. Then
> the lame shall leap like a deer, and the tongue
> of the dumb sing. For waters shall burst forth
> in the wilderness, and streams in the desert."
> (NKJV)

Notice how the healing power of God is described as *waters* breaking forth in the Wilderness and as streams in the desert. He describes it similarly again in Isaiah 43:19,

"Behold, I will do a new thing, now it shall spring forth; shall you not know it? I will even make a road in the wilderness and rivers in the desert." (NKJV)

So, God's power flowing to our problems is described as waters breaking out in the Wilderness. Now ask yourself, "Does the Bible also tell us specifically where these waters flow from?" Yes, in Ezekiel 47:1-9, the Bible describes these healing waters as flowing from the Temple of God and going down to the desert (which is the same as the Wilderness). Since the Temple is in the

Promised Land, the waters flowed from the Promised Land into the Wilderness.

Now put this all together with the Journey of Israel Map. God describes His power as waters flowing from the Promised Land into the Wilderness. When we walk in the Promised Land, His power will flow (from His Temple) like rivers of living water to our problems in the Wilderness. In other words, when we walk in the Spirit, His power flows to our problems in the flesh to heal, deliver, and provide for us.

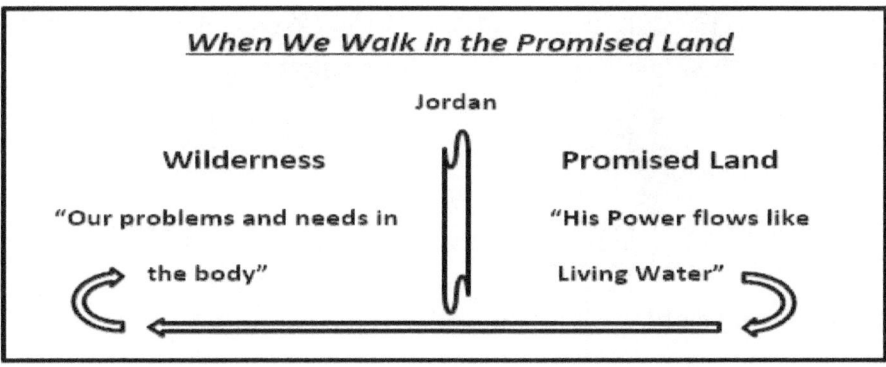

Who wouldn't want His healing, provision, and delivering power to flow like a river to the problems and circumstances that we face in this Wilderness? If we desire His power and provision in our lives, we must walk in the Promised Land. In other words, we have to walk in the Spirit.

Walking in the Spirit means that we are putting our flesh to death daily and "going forward" in faith, and that is where the river of His power flows. In Philippians 3:10, Paul said,

> "...that I may know Him and the power of His resurrection, and the fellowship of His

sufferings, being conformed to His death."
(NKJV)

Notice that when Paul spoke of *the power of His resurrection*, he also spoke of *being conformed to His death* because the two go hand in hand. If we want to know His power, we must also know the fellowship of His sufferings.

Why does Jesus teach us to forgive? Why does Jesus say to turn the other cheek? Why does He say that if someone takes your coat, give him your cloak also? Because He is teaching us to put the desires of our flesh to death and walk in the Spirit. He is teaching us to walk in the treasure of the Promised Land, for it is then that the Power of the Holy Spirit flows upon our present circumstances.

JESUS GAVE US THE EXAMPLE OF HIMSELF

Jesus is our example. The Bible says,

> "For to this you were called, because Christ also
> suffered for us, leaving us an example, that
> you should follow His steps: 'Who
> committed no sin, nor was deceit found in
> His mouth'; who, when He was reviled, did
> not revile in return; when He suffered, He did
> not threaten, but committed Himself to Him
> who judges righteously." (1st Peter 2:21-23
> NKJV)

He committed Himself to the Father. When He was on the

cross, He asked the Father to forgive the very ones that were killing Him. Then the Father raised Jesus from the dead through the power of the Holy Spirit.

Do you see the pattern? Jesus committed Himself to the Father, and the power of the Holy Spirit moved upon Him. Jesus laid His life down for us in love, and the Father raised Him from the dead through the power of the Holy Spirit. So also, following that same example, it is when we walk in the Spirit by loving others and taking up our cross and following Jesus, that the Holy Spirit will move upon our present circumstances. 2nd Chronicles 16:9 describes it this way,

> "For the eyes of the Lord run to and fro
>> throughout the whole earth, to show Himself
>> strong on behalf of those whose heart is loyal
>> to Him..." (NKJV)

When we walk in the treasure of the Promised Land, His power will flow to our problems while we are still in these earthen vessels in the Wilderness. We must choose to walk in the Promised Land instead of the Wilderness. In other words, we must choose to walk in the Spirit instead of the flesh. Only through the power of the Holy Spirit can we make that choice. We simply need to keep the faith and go forward on the path, the Staircase, that the Father has already provided.

CHAPTER 17

THE TABERNACLE "MAP"

IN THE LAST FEW CHAPTERS, WE HAVE BEEN LOOKING AT the Journey of Israel and how this entire journey served as a "map" of our Redemption in Christ. During that same Journey, God gave Moses another "map" that also spoke of our Redemption in Christ, and I will refer to this as the "Tabernacle Map."

After the Children of Israel departed from Egypt and arrived in the Wilderness, the Lord gave Moses the pattern of the Tabernacle and its furnishings. You'll remember that we looked at how the Menorah and the Ark (two pieces of furniture in the Tabernacle) served as a "map" of our Redemption. However, it was not only those two pieces of furniture, but also the entire structure of the Tabernacle that served as a map of our Redemption in Christ.

Both the "Tabernacle Map" and the "Journey of Israel Map" declare the same message of our Redemption that has been made available to us through Jesus, the Staircase. These two maps are direct parallels of one another, and they fit perfectly together to declare all that Jesus would come to accomplish.

THE TWO "MAPS" COMBINED

The "Tabernacle Map" consists of the Tabernacle Court and the Tent of Meeting. The court of the Tabernacle contained the Altar of Burnt Offering and the Laver, whereas, the Tent of Meeting (the main Tabernacle structure) held the Menorah, the Table of Showbread, the Altar of Incense, and the Ark of the Covenant, which stood behind the veil.

The Tabernacle

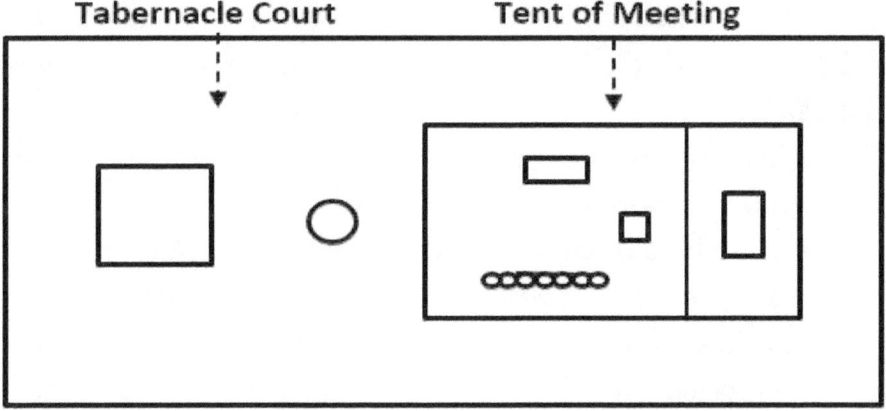

In the following illustration, you will see the "Journey of Israel Map" combined with the "Tabernacle Map," and how they correspond directly to each other. In combining the two maps, the Wilderness contains the Altar of Burnt Offering, the Jordan River contains the Laver, and the Promised Land contains the Tent of Meeting (which housed the Menorah and the Ark).

"The Two Maps Combined"

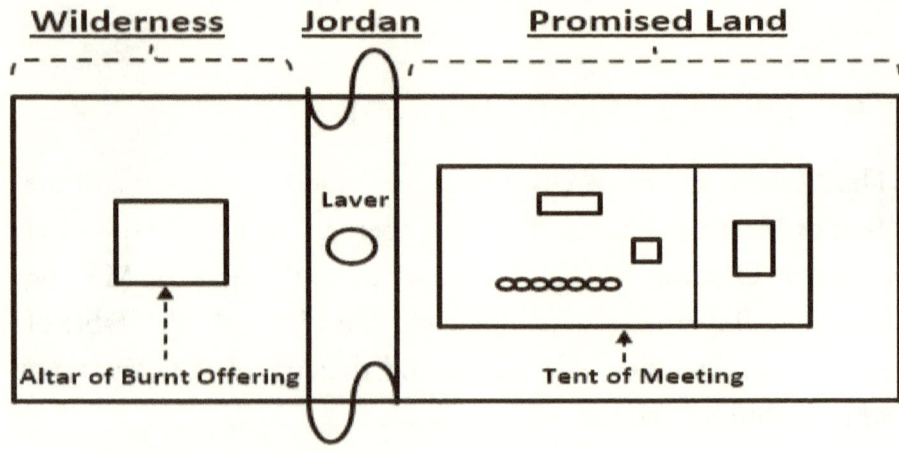

Wilderness   Jordan   Promised Land

Laver

Altar of Burnt Offering   Tent of Meeting

You will notice that in comparison to the Journey of Israel Map, the Tabernacle is only found in the regions of the Wilderness and the Promised Land, while no part of the Tabernacle is found in Egypt. That is because Egypt represents the bondage of sin and this world, and the Tabernacle represents our relationship with God as Christians.

Once we have believed in Jesus, we immediately depart from the sin and bondage of this world (Egypt) so that we can serve God in the Wilderness and the Promised Land. Only nonbelievers remain in Egypt, for nonbelievers have no part in the Tabernacle until they believe in Jesus. Therefore, the Tabernacle only lines up with the Wilderness and the Promised Land.

THE JORDAN AND THE LAVER

It is amazing to see how the Tabernacle tells the exact same message as the Journey of Israel. Just as the Jordan River is the starting point on the Journey of Israel Map, so the Laver is the starting point for a Christian on the Tabernacle Map, and they both declare our New Birth in Christ.

How do we know that the Laver is the starting point in the Tabernacle? We know this because God gave us this pattern when He instructed the priests to first wash in the Laver before ministering at either the Tent of Meeting or the Altar of Burnt Offering. Exodus 30:18-21 says,

> "You shall also make a laver of bronze, with its base also of bronze, for washing. You shall put it between the tabernacle of meeting and the altar. And you shall put water in it, for Aaron and his sons shall wash their hands and their feet in water from it. When they go into the tabernacle of meeting, or when they come near the altar to minister, to burn an offering made by fire to the Lord, they shall wash with water, lest they die. So they shall wash their hands and their feet, lest they die. And it shall be a statute forever to them—to him and his descendants throughout their generations." (NKJV)

As the priests would enter the court of the Tabernacle, before they went to either the Altar of Burnt Offering or the Tent of Meeting to do the service of the Tabernacle, the very first place they were instructed to go was the Laver. So, as they entered the Tabernacle, they would pass right by the Altar of Burnt Offering and go straight to the Laver to wash.

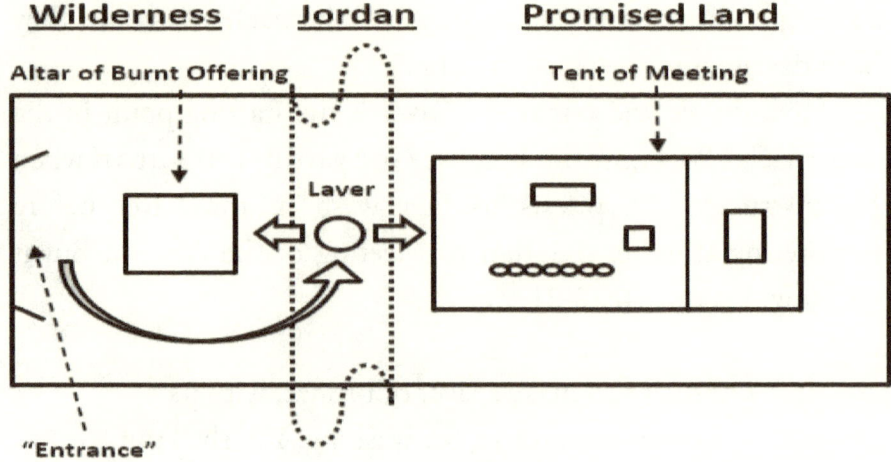

Now compare this to our Salvation in Christ. When we receive Jesus as our Savior, we are born again, which the Bible calls "the washing of regeneration" (Titus 3:5). Just like the Laver was the first place that the priests were to go, so also, on the Tabernacle Map, it is the first place that we find ourselves as we become Christians.

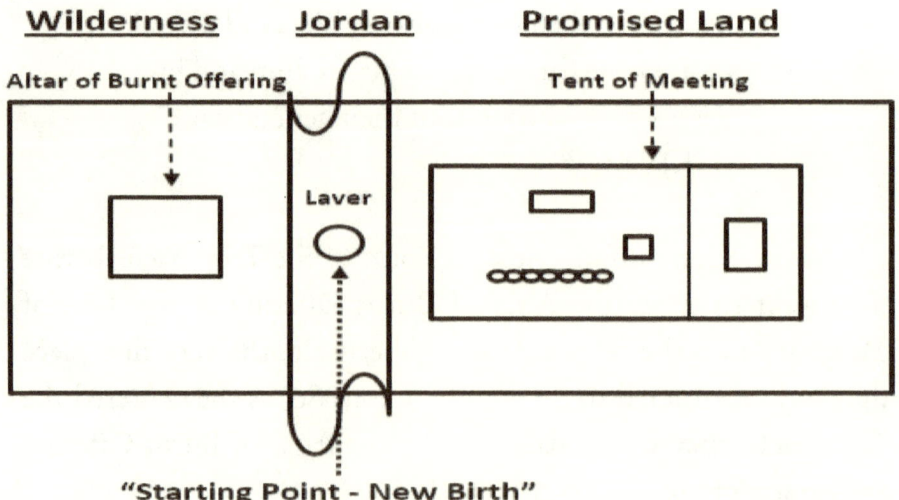

So, on this Tabernacle Map, once we receive Jesus as our Savior, we pass right by the Altar of Burnt Offering (because Jesus already fulfilled that which the burnt offering represents), and we go straight to the Laver which represents our new birth in Christ, the "washing" of regeneration.

You see, in combining the two maps, the Laver lines up directly with the Jordan River, and they both describe the day that we are born again and enter the position of being a Christian. In the Tabernacle Map, a new believer immediately goes past the Altar of Burnt Offering and finds himself at the Laver, and in the Journey of Israel Map, a new believer immediately crosses the Wilderness and finds himself at the Jordan.

THE ALTAR OF BURNT OFFERING AND THE WILDERNESS

In combining the two Maps, it is the Altar of Burnt Offering that correlates directly to the Wilderness. Just as the Wilderness represents the "Death of our flesh In Christ" and the remainder of our journey on this earth as Christians, so also the Altar of Burnt Offering declares the exact same message.

Jesus is the fulfillment of every offering and everything that the Altar of Burnt Offering represents. Yet after Jesus fulfilled it all, God also used the Altar of Burnt Offering to represent the Christian. In the New Testament, Paul tells us as Christians to present our bodies as a living sacrifice to God (Romans 12:1 NKJV). You see, Jesus has sanctified us through His blood and made us acceptable to God as a living sacrifice, symbolically speaking, upon the Altar of Burnt Offering.

The blood of Jesus cleanses us from all sin and makes us "... accepted in the Beloved" (Ephesians 1:6 NKJV), and it is only through Jesus that we could ever be referred to as a "living sacrifice." If we are not cleansed by His blood, then we are not acceptable for anything.

What is the Lord telling us with the Altar of Burnt Offering and the Wilderness lining up in these two maps? He is telling us that for the remainder of our journey on this earth, we need to put the deeds of the flesh to death daily and walk in the Spirit. In other words, we need to keep our body on this Altar of Burnt Offering as a living sacrifice to God.

As Christians, our body is dead in Christ, and it is our "reasonable service" to keep our body on this altar. In other words, it is simply our reasonable service to live for Jesus. We should not walk in the flesh (because it is dead in Christ). Instead, we are to walk in the Spirit (the Kingdom of God) by keeping our minds on Him. Romans 8:13 says,

> "For if you live according to the flesh you will die;
>   but if by the Spirit you put to death the deeds
>   of the body, you will live." (NKJV)

As Christians, if we keep our mind on the things of this world, it would be the same as taking our body off this Altar and living in the flesh again instead of living to God. It would be the same as turning our hearts back to the bondage of Egypt. On the other hand, it is when we keep our mind on the things of the Spirit that we are keeping our bodies on this Altar of Burnt Offering like a "living sacrifice" to God (Romans 12:1 NKJV).

THE TENT OF MEETING AND THE PROMISED LAND

In combining the Tabernacle Map with the Journey of Israel Map, it is the Tent of Meeting that correlates directly to the Promised Land. Both the Tent of Meeting and the Promised Land line up directly together, and both describe the position of "our spirit" after we have become Christians, for they declare that our spirit is made alive in Christ.

What is the Lord telling us with the Tent of Meeting and the Promised Land directly lining up in these two maps? He is telling us that as Christians, we are born again and can now walk in the unseen, invisible, all-powerful Kingdom of God.

LOOK AT THE PATTERN

Remember the principle that God established in the law, how that before the priests could minister at the Altar of Burnt Offering or the Tent of Meeting, they first had to wash at the Laver. This pattern is a picture of our Salvation in Christ.

Once we have been to the Laver (which represents our new birth), we are immediately invited into the Holy of Holies, which represents the very Presence of God and His Kingdom. This is that wonderful "Secret Place" which is spoken of in Psalm 91, "He who dwells in the secret place of the Most High shall abide under the shadow of the Almighty." Because of Jesus, we now have access to that Secret Place (the Kingdom of God) and can walk in the Spirit for the remainder of our journey on this earth as we put our flesh upon that Altar of Burnt Offering daily, being a living sacrifice to God.

SUMMARY OF THE TWO MAPS COMBINED

What is the Lord wanting us to see in combining these two maps? He wants us to see that the moment we receive Jesus as our Savior, we are born again. We immediately leave the bondage of the world and find ourselves washing at the Laver (on the Tabernacle Map) and the Jordan River (on the Journey of Israel Map). In other words, we find ourselves born again by the washing of regeneration and renewing of the Holy Spirit.

Both the Laver and the Jordan declare our initial faith in Christ. They declare the moment that we enter our position as a Christian, and that position is that "our flesh is dead in Christ," and "our spirit is made alive in Christ."

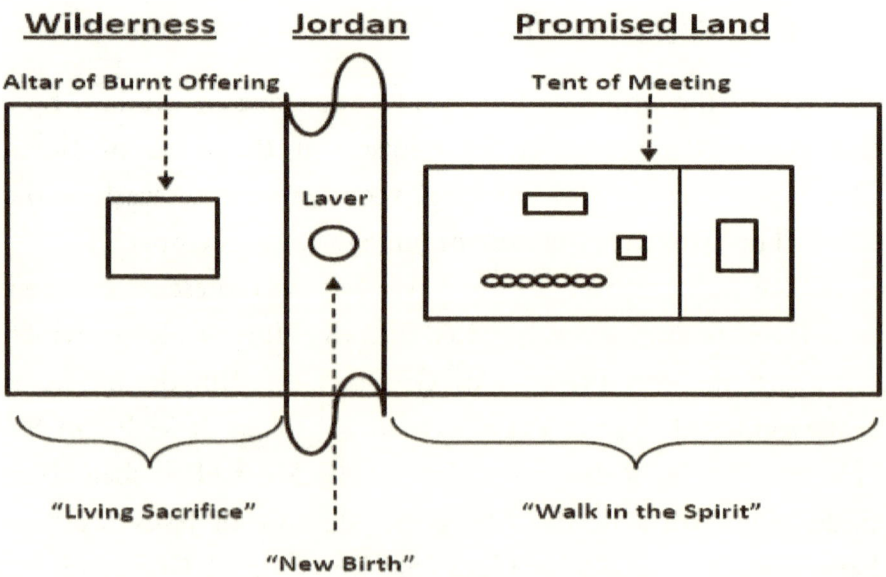

Therefore, these two maps not only declare our position as a Christian, but they also declare how we are to walk in that position for the remainder of our journey of faith upon this earth. How do we do this? By keeping our flesh on that Altar of Burnt Offering through the power of the Holy Spirit, thereby presenting our bodies as a "living sacrifice" to God. While at the same time, we keep our mind on the things of the Spirit, and walk forth in the unseen, invisible, all-powerful Kingdom of God.

CHAPTER 18

ALL THREE "MAPS" COMBINED

WE HAVE LOOKED AT THREE MAPS IN GOD'S WORD, AND all three of these maps fit perfectly together as one. The following is an illustration of all three maps combined.

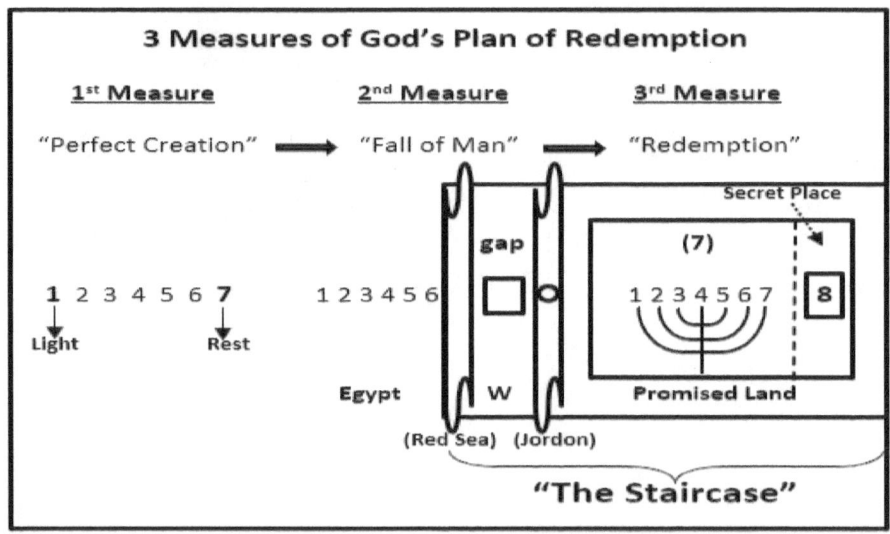

Whether it was the "3 Measures of God's Plan of Redemption Map," the "Journey of Israel Map," or the "Tabernacle Map," they all tell the same message of the Staircase, Jesus Christ, that brings us to the Father and allows us to walk in the Kingdom of God.

Notice the end result of each map. The 3 Measures Map ends with the 3rd Measure, "Redemption." The Journey of Israel Map ends with the "Promised Land," and the Tabernacle Map ends with the "Secret Place" (or Most Holy Place). All three endings are synonymous with one another, and all three reveal the unseen, invisible, all-powerful Kingdom of God that we have been invited into through the Staircase.

WHY "MAPS"?

Why does the Lord give us these maps and patterns to look at? It is because He wants us to be able to visualize, in this physical realm, that which we have been given access to in the spirit realm. Just like a map of a city will help you get an understanding of that city, the maps that the Lord has given to us in His Word help us to have a better understanding of the spirit realm that we cannot see.

They are simply maps of the spirit realm that help us to understand our true identity as Christians. Each map declares how, after we receive Jesus as our Savior, we enter our position as a new creation in Christ. Think about our position as Christians. Our flesh is dead in Christ, and our spirit is born again. The "old you" is no longer your identity. That is not who you are. Your identity now comes from who you are "in Christ." The Bible says that we have,

> "...put on the new man who is renewed in
> knowledge according to the image of Him
> who created him." (Colossians 3:10 NKJV)

He is now your identity. You are who He says you are and everything that He paid for you to be. We have put on the new man, and these maps help us to see that we are now free to walk in the Promised Land and dwell in the Secret Place. In other words, we are free to operate in the Kingdom of God.

THE "MAPS" ARE LIKE A MIRROR

James 1:22-24 says, "But be doers of the word, and not hearers only, deceiving yourselves. For if anyone is a hearer of the word and not a doer, he is like a man observing his natural face in a mirror, for he observes himself, goes away, and immediately forgets what kind of man he was" (NKJV).

The Bible says that God's Word is like a mirror. As Christians, we can look into the mirror of His Word and see the reflection of Jesus staring back at us. In other words, we can read His Word and find out that through Jesus, our old nature is dead, and the mirror of His Word shows us who we "Now" are in Christ.

These Maps work like a mirror in that same way. They help us to see that as Christians, even though we are still in the midst of this fallen world, we have been given access to the Kingdom of God through the Staircase, and we can now walk in the Spirit instead of the flesh.

Galatians 5:1 says, "Stand fast therefore in the liberty by

which Christ has made us free, and do not be entangled again with a yoke of bondage" (NKJV).

We have now been given the privilege to "walk" in the Promised Land and "dwell" in the Secret Place, which both represent the Kingdom of God. The question is, will I walk away from the mirror and forget who I am in Christ? Or am I going to walk in the Kingdom of God during the remainder of my journey of faith on this earth?

A DAILY CHOICE

How do we walk in the Kingdom of God? Remember that our walk is always determined by what we choose to keep our mind on. If we are going to walk in the Kingdom of God, it will be because we are keeping our mind on the things of the Spirit. Just as Isaiah 26:3 says,

> "You will keep him in perfect peace whose mind
> is stayed on you because he trusts in you."
> (NKJV)

We have a daily choice of whether we will keep our mind on the things of the Spirit that have been freely given to us, or the things of the flesh which have to do with our old nature. If we keep our mind on the things of the Spirit, we will walk in the Spirit, and if we keep our mind on the things of the flesh, we will walk in the flesh. Are we choosing to walk and dwell in the Spirit?

Psalm 91 starts off by saying, "He who dwells in the secret place of the Most High...," and then goes on to give the wonderful promises of God to the one who chooses to *dwell* there. You see, once we have become Christians, we have entered that Secret Place beyond the veil by His grace through faith, but are we choosing to *dwell* there daily? Are we choosing to keep our mind on God?

In that same way, we have entered the Promised Land by His grace through faith, but are we choosing to walk there every day? Or do we find ourselves turning our hearts back to Egypt, back to the things of the world, by letting our focus be on the things of our old nature?

Galatians 5:25 says, "if we live in the Spirit, let us also walk in the Spirit" (NKJV).

This scripture warns us that it is possible to live in the Spirit, but to "not" be walking there. As Christians, we now "live" in the spirit because we are born again, and that is our position in Christ, but are we choosing to "walk" in the Spirit? It is possible to live in the Spirit and find ourselves actually walking according to the flesh.

Also, in Ephesians 5:8, Paul says,

> "For you were once darkness, now you are light in
> the Lord. Walk as children of light." (NKJV)

Paul is saying that once we have been born again, we have passed from darkness to light. That is now our position in Christ, just as Jesus said that we are the light of the world. Paul then goes on to admonish us to *"walk"* as children of light.

So, we have the light, but are we walking in it? We have entered the Promised Land, but are we walking there? We have entered the Secret Place, but are we dwelling there? We have been given access to His Kingdom, but are we operating in it?

THE MAPS REVEAL THE PATTERN

There is a certain pattern and order that God puts forth with these maps, and He is showing us how things work in the spirit realm. The pattern is simply this: we should no longer walk in the ways of the flesh, which have already been put to death in Christ, but we should walk in the Spirit.

We are to walk in what God has freely given to us through the Finished Works of Christ, and then His power will flow to our circumstances in this world. His power flows as we walk in the pattern, but are we following the pattern of instruction that God has given to us?

GOD WANTS US TO DO THINGS HIS WAY

In 1st Chronicles (chapters 13 through 15), the Bible tells us of how King David tried to transport the Ark of the Covenant in his own way instead of following the pattern that the Lord had given. He chose to put the Ark on a new cart instead of having the Levites carry the Ark by poles on their shoulders, as the Lord had commanded Moses. Since he chose to do it his own way, it did not turn out well, and the Ark was turned aside to the field of Obed-Edom for three months (1st Chronicles 13:14).

Then David went back and commanded that the Ark be transported according to the "proper order" that God had instructed. When he did it according to the pattern, it was then that the Ark was brought to the city of David with great joy (1st Chronicles 15:12-25).

The message is clear, God wants us to do things His way instead of our own, and that is where we will find the moving of the Holy Spirit. The Holy Spirit moves upon God's Word, and it is our job to line up with His Word.

So, the maps reveal the pattern and declare that if we are going to walk in the Kingdom of God, then we must keep our mind on the things of the Spirit and put the deeds of the body to death daily (Colossians 3:1-7). These maps declare that His power will flow upon our problems as we abide in Him and keep the faith.

As we walk in the Promised Land, His power will flow to our problems in the Wilderness. As we dwell in the Secret Place, we will abide under the shadow of the Almighty. As we walk in the Kingdom of God, His power will flow upon our physical needs in this world.

The question is, are we walking according to the pattern that He laid out? Are we walking in the Promised Land and dwelling in the Secret Place by keeping our mind stayed on Him? Are we dying to the flesh daily and keeping our body upon that Altar as a living sacrifice to God?

ASK FOR HELP

God did not invite us into His glorious Kingdom without also giving us the power to walk there. In John 14:26, Jesus said that the Holy Spirit is our *Helper*. He did not leave us here alone. Whatever we are struggling with, or whatever it might be that is trying to keep us from walking in the Promised Land and dwelling in the Secret Place of His Presence daily, we just need to ask the Father to help us through the power of the Holy Spirit.

With help from the one whom the Father sent in the name of His Son, we will overcome it and prevail. We are to simply ask for

His help, and with the Holy Spirit helping us, we cannot fail. Jesus overcame the world and gave us the Holy Spirit so that we could also overcome all things through Him.

DON'T GO BACK TO YOUR OLD IDENTITY

Therefore, God gave us these maps to help us see our identity in Christ and all that is made available to us through the Staircase. Since the Promised Land Rest has been given to us, why wouldn't we want to walk there? Since the Secret Place has been made available to us, why wouldn't we want to dwell there? Since we have been invited into His glorious Kingdom, why wouldn't we want to operate in that Kingdom every day?

Why would we ever want to go back to the identity of our old nature instead of believing what the Word says concerning our new identity in Christ? Since it is Christ who now lives in us as Christians, why would we ever want to walk in less than who we really are in Christ? Don't turn again to the weakness and depravity of this world. You don't have to walk as the "old you" anymore. Your true identity is found in Jesus Christ.

CHAPTER 19

BE AWARE OF THE ENEMY'S TRICKS AND SCHEMES

"Be sober, be vigilant; because your adversary the
devil walks about like a roaring lion, seeking
whom he may devour. Resist him, steadfast in
the faith..." (1st Peter 5:8-9 NKJV)

A COACH OF A SPORTS TEAM KNOWS THAT ONE OF THE
best ways to help his team win the game is to make them
understand what their opponent is going to try and do to stop
them. It works a lot the same way with our Heavenly Father. Our
Heavenly Father desires for each of us to fully walk in all that has
been made available to us through Jesus, the Staircase. To help us
do this, He not only lets us know that there is an enemy who is
trying his best to stop us, but He also reveals his tactics.

God tells us that the enemy must seek out whom he can
devour. He has to look for those that he can devour because he
cannot devour those who are operating in the Kingdom of God.
If we will walk in the Kingdom of God and do things God's way

instead of our own, then the devil has no power to devour us because we are abiding in the Presence of God.

So, God warns us that in the remainder of our journey of faith on this earth, we need to be very aware of the tricks and schemes of the enemy, and we need to resist him in the faith. One of the enemy's biggest tricks is to get us so distracted with the ways of this world that we are no longer operating in the power of the Spirit that is available to us in Christ.

WHAT DOES THE ENEMY KNOW?

The enemy knows your potential as a Christian. He knows that you have the blood of Jesus and the power of the Holy Spirit. He knows that you have the power to walk in the Promised Land and to dwell in the Secret Place, which is the Kingdom of God. So, one of his primary goals is to try and keep you from walking in your full potential in Christ. The enemy wants to tempt you to walk in the flesh and to go back to your old ways, back to the "old you," so that you cannot function in the power of the Spirit.

As Christians, our flesh is dead in Christ, but the enemy will try to tempt you back into those things of the flesh that were already destroyed in Christ. Just as Paul describes in Galatians 2:18,

> "For if I build again those things which I
> destroyed, I make myself a transgressor."
> (NKJV)

The Bible clearly reveals why the enemy will do everything he can to get Christians to walk in the flesh and rebuild what Jesus already destroyed. It is so that we will grieve the Holy Spirit. In Ephesians 4:27, Paul admonishes us not to give place to the devil. Then he goes on to say,

> "And do not grieve the Holy Spirit of God, by
> whom you were sealed for the day of
> redemption. Let all bitterness, wrath, anger,
> clamor, and evil speaking be put away from
> you, with all malice. And be kind to one
> another, tenderhearted, forgiving one
> another, even as God in Christ forgave you."
> (Ephesians 4:30-32 NKJV)

God is saying that when we walk in the ways of the flesh, like bitterness, wrath, and anger, we are giving place to the devil because those kinds of actions result in grieving the Holy Spirit. Now think about this, if we are grieving the Holy Spirit, then God's power will not flow through us in the way that God wants it to. It's as if we are choosing those fleshly ways instead of God's Kingdom and Presence.

So, the enemy tries to distract us by bringing us back into the bondage of this world from which Christ has already set us free. Whenever we let things like lust, pride, bitterness, unforgiveness (or whatever the temptation may be) reign in our hearts, we have just given place to the devil.

You see, God's Word turns on the light and makes us aware of the tricks and schemes of the enemy so that we won't be tricked by him anymore. We have great potential in Christ, but the enemy tries to keep us from walking in that potential.

We are free from bondage and have been invited to walk in

the Promised Land, and to dwell in the Secret Place where all of God's power flows. Yet the enemy desires to have us so distracted with the ways of this world that we are no longer operating in the Kingdom of God. If he can accomplish that, then he can fight us instead of having to face the one who has already defeated him.

MAKE THE ENEMY FACE JESUS INSTEAD OF YOU

The battle is the Lord's, and Jesus has already won the victory. Jesus already defeated the devil when He came and stripped him of all power at the cross. The devil certainly knows the greatness of Jesus and that he has no power against Him.

So, when the enemy comes to fight you with his worldly distractions and temptations, just make him face the one who has already defeated Him, Jesus Christ. How? By lining up with the Word of God and doing things His way instead of our own.

The Bible admonishes us to put on the full armor of God so that we may be able to stand against the wiles of the devil (Ephesians 6:10-18). One piece of that armor is the sword of the Spirit which is the Word of God. Think about this. A sword was not made to just lay on the ground when the battle ensues. No, a sword was made to be handled. It's made to be picked up and used.

The sword of the Spirit works just the same. We have a daily choice to pick up the sword of the Spirit and use it. How do we pick it up? By believing His Word in our hearts and speaking it out of our mouths. When we believe and speak the Word of God, then we are making the enemy face the Word. The devil is always seeking an opportunity against us, and we simply need to raise our sword, which is the Word of God, and fight the good fight of faith.

Jesus is the mighty warrior in us that causes us to run at the giant just like David ran at Goliath. Just as Paul said,

> "I have been crucified with Christ; it is no longer I
> who live, but Christ lives in me; and the life
> which I now live in the flesh I live by faith in
> the Son of God, who loved me and gave
> Himself for me." (Galatians 2:20 NKJV)

When we yield ourselves to His Word by taking every thought captive to the obedience of Christ and by doing things His way instead of our own, that is when we are making the devil face Jesus instead of us. As we walk in the Promised Land and dwell in the Secret Place, we are, in essence hiding behind our hero, Jesus, who has already won the battle. He has already finished the work and will surely do what He has already done.

THE ENEMY TREMBLES AT THE PRESENCE OF JESUS

The enemy's motives are so easy to see when we understand that he trembles at the Presence of Jesus. When the enemy tries to tempt you with things like anger and unforgiveness, he is simply trying to get you to stop lining up with the Word by luring you back into the ways of the flesh. In other words, he is trying to get you to come out from behind Jesus so that he can fight you instead of facing the Word of God.

The Bible says that we are God's sheep and that we are

supposed to follow Jesus, our good Shepherd. To follow someone, you must be positioned "behind" the person you follow. It is when we are truly following Jesus that we are positioning ourselves behind Him, and that is when we make the enemy face Jesus instead of us. Always let Jesus face the enemy for you.

If the enemy can distract you and get you to willingly turn back to the ways of the "old you," he can beat you up all day. You're just falling for his tricks again. That's just the enemy's bait. If the devil can get you to walk in the flesh, you are simply no threat to him at all.

THE ENEMY WANTS TO SHIFT THE BATTLE

When I was about eleven years old, a friend and I went to see a high school football game, and I got myself into some trouble that I regretted. From the top of the bleachers, I decided that it would be fun to throw some pieces of popcorn down below onto some guys standing behind the bleachers. Those guys didn't like that idea, and as soon as I came down from the bleachers, this turned into a confrontation.

The one who was talking and confronting me with the issue was a big guy, and he asked me why I threw popcorn at him. Well, there was also another guy that was with him, and he was a lot younger and smaller than the big guy. So, I said to the big guy, "I wasn't throwing popcorn at you. I was throwing popcorn at him" (as I pointed to the smaller guy).

Suddenly, the whole battle "shifted" from being me against the big guy, to being me against the small guy. Thankfully, it ended peacefully, and I learned my lesson, but I was "shifting the battle" to my advantage. I knew I would be much better off confronting the small guy rather than the big guy.

You see, that is exactly how the enemy operates. He tries to shift the battle. He would much rather fight us (the small guy), than face Jesus, the Word, who has already defeated him. So, he tries to shift the battle to his advantage by getting us to walk in the flesh instead of the Spirit.

Think about it. If the devil can get us to act in fleshly ways like pride and arrogance, that is exactly how he fell from his position in Heaven in the first place. He would much rather have us grieve the Holy Spirit than to line up with the Word, where the battle has already been won by Jesus, and where the power of the Holy Spirit flows.

HOME FIELD ADVANTAGE

Sports teams always like to have the home field advantage. It's always much easier to play on their own field instead of someone else's. Just the same, the devil always wants home field advantage when he is going against us. He doesn't want to fight Christians on their home field, which is the Kingdom of God. No, he wants to get us down to his level, which is the fleshly ways of this world. That's his home field. If he can get us to operate in the flesh instead of the Spirit, then he has us right where he wants us. James 3:14-15 says,

> "But if you have bitter envy and self-seeking in
> your hearts, do not boast and lie against the
> truth. This wisdom does not descend from

above, but is earthly, sensual, demonic."
(NKJV)

If we act in bitter envy and strife, then we are acting like the devil himself. James goes on to contrast this *earthly* wisdom with the wisdom that is from above and says,

> "But the wisdom that is from above is first pure,
> then peaceable, gentle, willing to yield, full of
> mercy and good fruits, without partiality and
> without hypocrisy." (James 3:17 NKJV)

If we are acting like the devil instead of acting on God's wisdom from above, then we are certainly not going to be operating in the Kingdom of God. The moment we step over into the ways of the flesh, we have just let the devil bring us into his home field instead of making him come to our home field, the Kingdom of God, where he has no power at all.

We must be wise to line up with Jesus and follow the pattern that He has laid out in the maps of the spirit realm that are found in His Word. We need to do things His way instead of our own, and it is then that we are walking in the Promised Land and dwelling in the Secret Place. It is then that we are operating in the Kingdom that has been freely given to us.

IT'S NOT A PHYSICAL BATTLE

The enemy tries to make us think that it's a physical battle, but it's not. It is a spiritual battle. Ephesians 6:12 says,

> "For we do not wrestle against flesh and blood,
>> but against principalities, against powers,
>> against the rulers of the darkness of this age,
>> against spiritual hosts of wickedness in the
>> heavenly places." (NKJV)

So, the Bible clearly tells us that the battle is not in the physical realm that we see, but instead in the unseen realm of principalities, powers, and spiritual hosts of wickedness.

Yet, the enemy always tries his hardest to make us think that the battle is in the physical realm. He tries to make us think that "people" are the enemy. But those people, whom the devil is trying to get us to hate and to fight with, are the very people whom Christ died for. Those are the very people that God wants us to forgive and pray for so that they can also come out of the devil's bondage and receive what Jesus has done for them before it's too late. 2nd Timothy 2:24-26 says,

> "And a servant of the Lord must not quarrel but
>> be gentle to all, able to teach, patient, in
>> humility correcting those who are in
>> opposition, if God perhaps will grant them
>> repentance, so that they may know the truth,
>> and that they may come to their senses and
>> escape the snare of the devil, having been
>> taken captive by him to do his will." (NKJV)

We need to be wise and not keep falling for the same tricks of the devil, who would have us think that people are the enemy. The devil is the real enemy, and we need to go after the real enemy through the power of the Holy Spirit. It is when we walk in the love of Jesus toward others that we are going after the real enemy.

DON'T FALL FOR THE DECOY

Picture yourself at sea on a battleship. Over to one side, you see an entire fleet of ships ready to attack you. With the dread of this ensuing attack approaching, you turn all your guns and all your strength and energy over toward this oncoming attack. Then come to find out, those ships which you thought were about to attack you were just decoys sent out by the "real enemy." The real enemy was approaching from the opposite direction to attack you while your back was turned.

You see, that's precisely how the devil works. If he can get us to fight in the flesh, and make us think that people are the enemy, then we'll spend all our strength and energy fighting a decoy while the devil is pounding us from the back. But when we listen to God's Word, and we do it His way instead, by walking in love and forgiveness, that's when we turn our weapons right at the real enemy (the devil), and we make him face the one who has already defeated him.

DISTRACTIONS ARE NOT WORTH IT

Is there anything more important than God's Presence flowing in our lives? Of course not. Every day we need to ask ourselves why we would ever let the ways of the flesh distract us from the greatness of Jesus, who has overcome it all. Our relationship with the Lord is far more critical and way too precious, than to let some meaningless flesh-driven emotion draw us away from the treasure of His Presence.

Next time you have an opportunity to act in the flesh, ask yourself, "Is this really worth it?" When we act in the flesh, we stop God from fighting our battles for us in the way He wants to. Is it really worth it to let your actions stop the Holy Spirit from doing what He wants to do in the situation? If we are grieving the Holy Spirit by choosing anger instead of forgiveness, how is His power going to flow in our lives in the way that He wants it to?

If we are grieving the Holy Spirit, how is that pursuing more of His Presence in our life? How is that seeking the Kingdom of God first? When you start measuring things up that way, it starts getting easy to see how petty, small, and meaningless the things of this world are. Nothing is important enough to get in the way of God's Presence in our life. Proverbs 4:5 says,

> "Get wisdom! Get understanding! Do not forget,
> nor turn away from the words of my mouth."
> (NKJV)

As Christians, we still have a daily choice of how we are going to walk out this journey of faith for the remainder of our time on this earth. We need to stop letting the enemy distract us and choose to do it God's way instead. Why would we ever let the enemy distract us from walking in the victory of the Kingdom of God that our great Lord and King Jesus has already won?

ONE THING IS NEEDED

There are so many distractions in this world, but as Jesus said to Martha regarding her sister Mary who was sitting at His feet and listening to His Word, "One thing is needed..." (Luke 10:39-42 NKJV). The message was very clear. Martha was distracted, but Mary had her full attention on Jesus and was determined not to let anything get in the way of that. Jesus saw Mary's heart and would not let that be taken away from her.

Mary had gotten a hold of that "one thing" that is needed, for she realized that all she needed was a relationship with Jesus. By giving her full attention to Jesus, her actions showed that she understood the absolute greatness of this mighty man, the Son of God, who stood before her.

CHAPTER 20

THE GREATNESS OF JESUS

"Great is the Lord, and greatly to be praised. His greatness is unsearchable." (Psalm 145:3)

From the first page to the last, the entire Old Testament was all about Jesus. It was like a blueprint of the Staircase that Jacob saw in the dream, and Jesus is that Staircase. The Father made it so clear that there is only one way to Him, and that way is Jesus. The Old Testament was simply a testimony of the greatness of His Son.

Consider the greatness of this one man whom the Father exemplified as being the Staircase that leads to Heaven, the only path to the Father. This one man who made all the difference. The man whom God foretold of in the garden of Eden as being the promised Seed who was coming to deliver us. The last Adam, the second Man, who came to win back all that the first man lost.

Consider the greatness of Jesus and the power of His Word. He was before all things, and in Him, all things consist. He left his home in Heaven and came down to earth. He lived a perfect life and is the lamb that was slain. The stone rolled away, and He rose on the 3rd day and became the firstborn from the dead that He might have pre-eminence in all things.

He calmed the sea and walked on top of it. He fed the multitudes, healed the sick, raised the dead, cast out demons, and caused them to tremble at His presence. He delivered us from all the oppression of the devil and stripped him of all power. He's the one who is worshipped and adored by all the angels in Heaven, and their desire is to look into the things concerning Him.

Consider the absolute greatness of this one man whom the entire Bible was written about, and He is the one who fulfills it all. The one who came to do His Father's will and finish His work. The one in whom all of God's prophecies, types and shadows, numbers, patterns, and symbols come together into one glorious, magnificent picture to declare that He alone is the Messiah and Christ, the Son of the living God. The one who is the same yesterday, today, and forever. The author and finisher of our faith. The Great I Am. He's the Alpha and the Omega, the beginning and the end, and He's the one who is coming again.

The one who, in His great mercy, paid the price for all our sins so that we could receive the precious, precious gift of the Holy Spirit and have His Presence abiding in us, making it possible for us to walk in the Promised Land and dwell in the Secret Place for the remainder of our journey of faith on this earth. No matter what struggles you are facing, always remember to consider the greatness of Jesus, the one who has already overcome it all.

DECLARE HIS GREATNESS WITH WORSHIP

The greatness of Jesus is so far above all that we could ever imagine that we simply need to come to Him with a heart of worship. Our minds can't even comprehend the infinite magnitude of our Lord and Savior, yet we can keep our mind on Him and give our full attention to Him as we worship Him.

If we truly desire to walk in the Promised Land and dwell in the Secret Place of His Presence, if we truly desire to walk in the Kingdom of God, then we need to constantly keep our mind on Jesus with a heart of thanksgiving and praise. One of the best ways to worship Him is to declare His greatness (Psalm 145:6 NKJV).

When the enemy tries to attack you and distract you, just start talking about the greatness of the one who already defeated him. The more that we declare the greatness of Jesus and praise His name, the more that we will put ourselves into a position for the Holy Spirit to flow into our lives.

WORSHIP INVITES THE GREATNESS OF JESUS INTO YOUR SITUATION

A heart of worship will take you deeper into the Presence of God and His Kingdom, and when you spend time in His Presence is when the greatness of Jesus will flow upon your circumstances in this world. He will hide you in the Secret Place of His Presence (Psalm 31:20), and it is in that place that you will find strength over the distractions of the enemy. It is in that place that His power will flow to your problems as you cast your cares upon Him.

Remember that it was when Paul and Silas were praying and singing to God, that suddenly there was a great earthquake, immediately the prison doors were opened, and their chains were loosed (Acts 16:25-26). Right in the midst of that terrible jail cell, they came before the Presence of God with a song of praise. Though they were physically bound, God's Word is never bound. So, it was as they sang, that suddenly the doors were unlocked, and their chains were loosed. Praise ushered in that "suddenly" moment of breakthrough.

We should always continue to worship God and give thanks, and in due season we will find ourselves in that "suddenly" moment of breakthrough when the greatness of Jesus breaks through upon our present circumstances.

King David was a man after God's own heart, and he certainly knew the importance of worship. In Psalm 34:1, He said,

> "I will bless the Lord at all times, and His praise
> shall continually be in my mouth." (NKJV)

King David used the words, *at all times*, and *continually*, because he knew that one of the secrets of being in God's Presence is to have a heart that is constantly filled with praise.

In Psalm 100:4, the Bible even gives us instructions as to how we should enter His Presence,

> "Enter into His gates with thanksgiving, and into
> His courts with praise. Be thankful to Him,
> and bless His name." (NKJV)

Jesus gave us this same type of example when He taught the disciples how to pray. His example prayer starts off with worship when He said,

> "...Our Father in Heaven, Hallowed be Your
> name." (Luke 11:2 NKJV)

The word *hallowed* is an adjective that means "greatly revered and honored." Jesus was teaching us how to approach the Father and be in His Presence. So, when we come to the Lord, it should always be with an attitude of worship and thanksgiving.

PRAISE IS BEAUTIFUL

In Psalm 147:1, the Bible says that "Praise is beautiful." So, God declares that our praise is beautiful to Him. Our mighty God is self-sufficient and certainly needs nothing from anyone. Yet He is so compassionate as to make a way for us to be able to bring something to Him, and that He would even call it *beautiful.*

Think of how merciful and gracious He is even to allow the words of our lips to come into His ears, and that He would count our worship and thanksgiving as valuable to Himself. He even says that His "inmost being will rejoice when our lips speak right things" (Proverbs 23:16 NKJV).

Think about a bride on her wedding day. She desires to be just as beautiful as she can possibly be for her bridegroom. As the bride of Christ, we should certainly desire to be just as beautiful as we can be for our bridegroom Jesus as we live out our daily lives and anticipate His soon return. If we have a heart that desires to be as beautiful as we can possibly be for Jesus, then we need to have a heart of worship.

THE SIMPLICITY OF WORSHIP

There is a beautiful simplicity in worship that God wants us to get a hold of. God is complex in all His ways and past finding out (Romans 11:33), yet He made it simple for us. In 2nd Corinthians 11:3, Paul admonishes us and says,

> "But I fear, lest somehow, as the serpent deceived Eve by his craftiness, so your minds may be corrupted from the simplicity that is in Christ." (NKJV)

I love that word *simplicity* because God is so complex and far above us that it cannot be measured, yet He birthed a plan of pure simplicity through the Lord Jesus for our sake. So that we can simply receive Jesus by faith, and then continue in the faith by having a heart of worship and thanksgiving for who He is and all that He has done.

A heart of worship will keep you in that Secret Place of His Presence where you can hear God and have wonderful fellowship with Him. Then God, in the complexity of His great power, will flow upon our present circumstances and problems like a beautiful river of water giving life to a dry desert.

All of God's "maps" in His Word point us to this type of lifestyle of thanksgiving and praise, and they are the "how to" when it comes to walking in the Kingdom of God. Do you want the power of God in your life? Then do it His way by keeping your mind on Him and having a heart of worship that constantly declares the greatness of His Son Jesus.

AN INTENTIONAL HEART OF PRAISE

There are many times that we might not feel like keeping our mind on Jesus, worshipping, and giving thanks. Yet if we want to walk in the Promised Land and dwell in the Secret Place, if we want to operate in His Kingdom, then we must do what the Bible says and gird up the loins of our mind (1st Peter 1:13). We must stir up the gift of God that is in us (2nd Timothy 1:6) and do it anyway.

God wants to develop in each of us an intentional heart of praise; a heart that chooses to always worship on purpose and even when we don't feel like it. Just as Paul admonishes us to pray *always* with all prayer and supplication "in the Spirit" (Ephesians 6:18 NKJV). The Holy Spirit is right there to help us, and it is amazing how this works, but when we put forth the effort to praise the Lord even when we don't feel like it, then the Holy Spirit will move upon our effort of faith and help us.

There are many great scriptures in the Bible regarding worship, and it's always good to have a "go to" Bible verse that helps you get into an attitude of worship. For me, that verse is Revelation 4:8, which declares the very words that the Bible says are constantly being spoken in Heaven before His throne,

"Holy, Holy, Holy, Lord God Almighty who was and is and is to come."

It is amazing to think about the fact that every time you say this verse, you have just lined yourself up with the exact words of worship that are being spoken in Heaven before God's Throne at that very moment. This is a great verse to start speaking, even when you don't feel like worshipping. As you put forth the effort of faith to give praise intentionally, then the Holy Spirit will move upon your effort of faith as He develops in you an intentional heart of praise.

WITH THE MEASURE YOU USE

Jesus said that with the same measure we use, it will be measured back to us (Mark 4:24). That is a principle of His Kingdom that can be applied in many ways. When you apply this spiritual principle to worship, it becomes clear that in the same measure you decide to keep your mind on Jesus and worship Him, will be the same measure that you will walk and dwell in His Presence.

What is the measure of your worship and thanksgiving to God? He lets us choose the measure that we will use. For example, if we dip a spoon into a well of water, we will receive the measure of a spoon full of water. Yet if we dip a cup into that same well, we will receive the greater measure of a cup of water. What measure are we using in the Kingdom of God? What measure are we using as we draw water from the wells of Salvation that Jesus has freely given to us to draw from?

In the remainder of our journey of faith on this earth, it is now our divine privilege to seek after and "draw" from His Presence daily. Yet the measure that we use is our choice, and with the measure that we use, it will be measured back to us. We should always inspect ourselves as to how much time we spend worshipping Jesus and declaring His greatness. If we remember to constantly worship God and pray in the Spirit, then we will win every time.

CHOOSE THE STAIRCASE

What's the state of your heart if your life was to end tonight? The Staircase, Jesus Christ, the great Pathway of Deliverance, has been made available to all who choose to believe. Yet those who refuse Him are choosing the path of destruction. Just as Jesus said,

> "Enter by the narrow gate; for wide is the gate
> and broad is the way that leads to
> destruction, and there are many who go in
> by it. Because narrow is the gate and
> difficult is the way which leads to life, and
> there are few who find it." (Matthew 7:13-
> 14 NKJV)

When you choose to believe in Jesus, you are walking up the steps of this glorious Staircase that immediately brings you out of the bondage of this fallen world and straight into the wonderful Presence of God. Remember that Jesus said,

> "In the world you shall have tribulation, but be of
> good cheer, I have overcome the world."
> (John 16:33 NKJV)

Why can we be of good cheer? Because Jesus, the one who has already overcome it all, invites us to come to Him with everything, and He will take care of it. Jesus is greater than any problem we could ever face or imagine, and He is the answer to every problem.

What problems are you facing? Is it sickness? He is the healer. Is it financial trouble? He is the provider. Are you suffering from depression? In His Presence is fullness of joy. His Presence and Kingdom in your life will chase away the depression, just as light chases away the darkness, but we must know and believe that He is the deliverer. He said,

> "Call upon me in the day of trouble, I will deliver you, and you shall glorify me." (Psalm 50:15 *NKJV)*

He didn't say that He might deliver you. He said *I will deliver you.* But are we calling upon Him in a fashion of going after Him with all our heart? He is waiting for us to call upon Him on those lines. In an earnestness of seeking after Him like the greatness of the treasure that He is. A fervent desire to walk in the Promised Land and to dwell in the Secret Place by keeping our mind stayed on Him with a heart of worship.

His Presence is experienced as we are presently and daily pursuing Jesus and abiding in Him. Jesus said, "If you abide in Me, and My words abide in you, you will ask what you desire, and it shall be done unto you" (John 15:7 NKJV). He wants us to go after Him with all of our heart every day. That is what walking in the Kingdom of God truly is. It is a daily relationship with Jesus.

What could be more exciting than pursuing more of His Presence in our life every day, as we patiently wait for the Presence of His soon return? Why not go to sleep every night and wake up every day with that goal in mind, that you want more of Him in your life? There is nothing more worthwhile, and nothing more fulfilling, rewarding, and exciting than to persistently pursue more and more of Jesus.

LET HIM TAKE YOU BY THE HAND

If anyone does not believe that Jesus is the Son of God who came in the flesh, paid the price for our sins on the cross, and rose from the grave on the 3rd day through the power of the Holy Spirit, then it is only because they have not read and studied the Bible with a heart that sincerely wants to know the truth. If anyone will sincerely seek the truth, then they will certainly find Jesus.

If you have never received Jesus as your Lord and Savior, He loves you and is waiting for you. He is the way. Don't let your heart be bitter. If you've shunned the faith, then please reconsider. There's water to drink. Are you becoming thirsty? Just reach out your hand, don't forsake your own mercy.

Through Him, there is a bright road ahead, but the future will be what you choose. His present for you leaves all the past behind you. It's there to receive. It's on the table right now. It's been there for years; you just haven't seen it somehow. Have you walked enough of this world without Him? Have you lived enough of this life without Him? He is waiting for you.

The Bible says that if we confess with our mouth the Lord Jesus and believe in our heart that God raised Him from the dead, we will be saved. Please don't wait until it is too late. The Bible says to "Seek the Lord while He may be found, call upon Him while He is near" (Isaiah 55:6 KJV).

Don't let your chances slip away. He's calling you today. He is reaching down right now, ready to pull you out of the sinking sands of this life. He is simply waiting for you to reach out your hand of faith, and He will take you by the hand.

> "For I, the Lord your God, will hold your right
> hand, saying to you, 'Fear not, I will help
> you.'" (Isaiah 41:13 NKJV)

ACKNOWLEDGMENTS

Thank you to everyone at Publish Authority, you helped me so much and made the process so enjoyable! Special thanks to Frank and Bernadette Eastland and Bob and Nancy Laning on the Publish Authority team. What a wonderful group of believers to work with!

Special thanks to Raeghan Rebstock at Raeghan Designs for all your help with the book cover design, logo, and ministry website design. Thank you for your Godly wisdom and guidance throughout the entire process!

Special thanks to my entire family for your faith in the Lord, your constant love and encouragement, and for all of your help, not only on this book, but also throughout my whole life!

ABOUT THE AUTHOR

Matt Rankin is a singer/songwriter who has spent most of his life in the music business. His greatest passion, however, is his relationship with Jesus Christ. With over 30 years of devoted study of the Bible, Matt has answered God's call to write and proclaim the greatness of the one Man who is the only pathway to heaven in his book *Jesus Is The Staircase*. Matt and his wife, Nichole, are the founders of Stay Ready Ministry— a ministry that is dedicated to helping others to not only get ready for the return of Jesus Christ by receiving Him as Lord and Savior but to also **Stay Ready** through a passionate daily relationship with Him.

For more about Matt and his and Nichole's ministry, you are invited to visit their website at StayReadyMinistry.com.

www.ingramcontent.com/pod-product-compliance
Lightning Source LLC
Chambersburg PA
CBHW021626120626
46545CB00002B/416